Ancient Texts and the Bible
Book 10 - Easy Reader Edition

Israel...
Through the Book of Joshua

Minister 2 Others

Ancient Texts and the Bible
Book 10

Israel...
Through the Book of Joshua

Easy Reader Edition

Israel... Through the Book of Joshua
ISBN 978-1-947751-39-2

Ancient texts compiled for this series:

The Bible
King James Version 1769

The Book of Enoch
An English translation by Dr. Laurence,
Archbishop of Cashel,
Formerly Professor of Hebrew at Oxford, 1833

The Book of Jasher
Faithfully translated 1840
from the original Hebrew into English
Published by J.H. Parry & Company 1887

The Book of Jubilees
by R.H. Charles, Oxford: Clarendon Press, 1913

Ancient Texts and the Bible
series include:

Book 1: In The Beginning... From Adam to Noah

Book 2: In The Beginning... From Noah to Abraham

Book 3: In The Beginning... From Abraham to Israel

Book 4: In The Beginning... From Israel to Egypt

Book 5: In The Beginning... From Egypt to Goshen

Book 6: Israel... From Goshen to Sinai

Book 7: Israel... From Sinai to the Tabernacle

Book 8: Israel... Through the Book of Leviticus

Book 9: Israel... Through the Book of Numbers

Book 10: Israel... Through the Book of Joshua

Table of Contents:

Forward

The **Ancient Texts and the Bible** series synchronizes the manuscripts of Enoch, Jasher, and Jubilees into the Bible, making one complete storyline. The books are interwoven using the Torah as the backbone, and the extra-biblical texts as the fleshing out of that backbone.

The last book in this series contains parts of Deuteronomy chapters 31 & 34, the entire book of Joshua, and the book of Jasher chapters 87 through 91, as well as the book of Enoch chapter 91.

Though the language in the writings have been updated, replacing words like "*thou*" and "*thine*" with words like "*you*" and "*your*", the integrity of the verses remain.

The "*Easy Reader*" edition is for those who just want to read the storyline and enjoy the journey. The stop signs and complex formatting have been removed so one may merely focus upon the story being told.

The *Expanded Edition* of **Ancient Texts and the Bible** was created for the more studious reader. The various manuscripts have the following formatting applied to them in this edition:

the Bible - Regular

THE BOOK OF ENOCH - ALL CAPITALS

the Book of Jasher - Italics

the Book of Jubilees - Underlined

Where one of the extra-biblical texts reiterates the Bible, the phrase is then put in a **bold font**. Where two manuscripts overlap each other exclusive of the Bible, then both fonts are used. For instance, where Jasher and Jubilees intercept, the text is then formatted as *Italics and Underlined.*

The stop sign is another element to the *Expanded Edition* that is not seen in the *Easy Reader*. This image points to contradictions in the content. Printed versions also contain page numbers within the stop sign revealing the page where contradictory information is located, and vice versa. This information was not feasible to place in the e-book versions since the page numbers vary depending on the font size the reader chooses. Following, is an example from each edition:

Easy Reader Edition:

(Deuteronomy 34:5) (...Jasher 87:10)
So Moses the servant of the LORD died there in the land of Moab, according to the word of the LORD, in the fortieth year from the Israelites going forth from the land of Egypt.

Expanded Edition:

(Deuteronomy 34:5) *(...Jasher 87:10)*
So **Moses** the servant of the LORD **died there in the land of Moab, according to the word of the LORD,** *in the fortieth year from the Israelites going forth from the land of Egypt.*

Whichever you choose, may you ***Enjoy the Journey***!

Prologue

(Deuteronomy 31:14) (Jasher 87:1)

And at that time the LORD said to Moses, Behold, your days approach an end that you must die: call and take now Joshua the son of Nun your servant, and present yourselves and place him in the tabernacle of the congregation, that I may give him a charge. And Moses did so. And Moses and Joshua went, and presented themselves in the tabernacle of the congregation.

(Deuteronomy 31:15) (Jasher 87:2)

And the LORD appeared in the tabernacle in a pillar of a cloud: and the pillar of the cloud stood over the door at the entrance of the tabernacle.

(Deuteronomy 31:16)

And the LORD said to Moses, Behold, you shall sleep with your fathers; and this people will rise up, and go a whoring after the gods of the strangers of the land, whither they go to be among them, and will forsake me, and break my covenant which I have made with them.

(Deuteronomy 31:17)

Then my anger shall be kindled against them in that day, and I will forsake them, and I will hide my face from them, and they shall be devoured, and many evils and troubles shall befall them; so that they will say in that day, Are not these evils come upon us, because our God is not among us?

(Deuteronomy 31:18)

And I will surely hide my face in that day for all the evils which they shall have wrought, in that they are turned to other gods.

(Deuteronomy 31:19)
Now therefore write this song for you, and teach it the children of Israel: put it in their mouths, that this song may be a witness for me against the children of Israel.

(Deuteronomy 31:20)
For when I shall have brought them into the land which I swore to their fathers, that flows with milk and honey; and they shall have eaten and filled themselves, and waxen fat; then will they turn to other gods, and serve them, and provoke me, and break my covenant.

(Deuteronomy 31:21)
And it shall come to pass, when many evils and troubles are befallen them, that this song shall testify against them as a witness; for it shall not be forgotten out of the mouths of their seed: for I know their imagination which they go about, even now, before I have brought them into the land which I swore.

(Deuteronomy 31:22)
Moses therefore wrote this song the same day, and taught it the children of Israel.

(Deuteronomy 31:23) (Jasher 87:3)
And the Lord commanded Joshua the son of Nun and gave him a charge and said to him, Be strong and of a good courage: for you shall bring the children of Israel into the land which I swore to them: and I will be with you.

(Jasher 87:4)
And Moses said to Joshua, Be strong and courageous, for you will make the children of Israel inherit the land, and the Lord

will be with you, he will not leave you nor forsake you, be not afraid nor disheartened.

(Deuteronomy 31:24)

And it came to pass, when Moses had made an end of writing the words of this law in a book, until they were finished,

(Deuteronomy 31:25)

That Moses commanded the Levites, which bare the ark of the covenant of the LORD, saying,

(Deuteronomy 31:26)

Take this book of the law, and put it in the side of the ark of the covenant of the LORD your God, that it may be there for a witness against you.

(Deuteronomy 31:27)

For I know your rebellion, and your stiff neck: behold, while I am yet alive with you this day, you have been rebellious against the LORD; and how much more after my death?

(Deuteronomy 31:28)

Gather to me all the elders of your tribes, and your officers, that I may speak these words in their ears, and call heaven and earth to record against them.

(Deuteronomy 31:29)

For I know that after my death you will utterly corrupt yourselves, and turn aside from the way which I have commanded you; and evil will befall you in the latter days; because you will do evil in the sight of the LORD, to provoke him to anger through the work of your hands.

(Jasher 87:5)
And Moses called to all the children of Israel and said to them, You have seen all the good which the Lord your God has done for you in the wilderness.

(Jasher 87:6)
Now therefore observe all the words of this law, and walk in the way of the Lord your God, turn not from the way which the Lord has commanded you, either to the right or to the left.

(Jasher 87:7)
And Moses taught the children of Israel statutes and judgments and laws to do in the land as the Lord had commanded him.

(Jasher 87:8)
And he taught them the way of the Lord and his laws; behold they are written upon the book of the law of God which he gave to the children of Israel by the hand of Moses.

(Deuteronomy 31:30)
And Moses spoke in the ears of all the congregation of Israel the words of this song, until they were ended.

(Jasher 87:9)
And Moses finished commanding the children of Israel, and the Lord said to him, saying, Go up to the Mount Abarim and die there, and be gathered to your people as Aaron your brother was gathered.

~ ~ ~

(Deuteronomy 34:1) (Jasher 87:10...)

And Moses went up as the Lord had commanded him, from the plains of Moab to the mountain of Nebo, to the top of Pisgah, that is over against Jericho. And the LORD shewed him all the land of Gilead, to Dan,

(Deuteronomy 34:2)

And all Naphtali, and the land of Ephraim, and Manasseh, and all the land of Judah, to the utmost sea,

(Deuteronomy 34:3)

And the south, and the plain of the valley of Jericho, the city of palm trees, to Zoar.

(Deuteronomy 34:4)

And the LORD said to him, This is the land which I swore to Abraham, to Isaac, and to Jacob, saying, I will give it to your seed: I have caused you to see it with your eyes, but you shall not go over there.

(Deuteronomy 34:5) (...Jasher 87:10)

So Moses the servant of the LORD died there in the land of Moab, according to the word of the LORD, in the fortieth year from the Israelites going forth from the land of Egypt.

(Deuteronomy 34:6)

And he buried him in a valley in the land of Moab, over against Bethpeor: but no man knows of his sepulchre to this day.

(Deuteronomy 34:7)

And Moses was an hundred and twenty years old when he died: his eye was not dim, nor his natural force abated.

(Deuteronomy 34:8) (Jasher 87:11)

And the children of Israel wept for Moses in the plains of Moab thirty days: so the days of weeping and mourning for Moses were ended.

(Deuteronomy 34:9)

And Joshua the son of Nun was full of the spirit of wisdom; for Moses had laid his hands upon him: and the children of Israel hearkened to him, and did as the LORD commanded Moses.

(Deuteronomy 34:10)

And there arose not a prophet since in Israel like to Moses, whom the LORD knew face to face,

(Deuteronomy 34:11)

In all the signs and the wonders, which the LORD sent him to do in the land of Egypt to Pharaoh, and to all his servants, and to all his land,

(Deuteronomy 34:12)

And in all that mighty hand, and in all the great terror which Moses shewed in the sight of all Israel.

Joshua: Chapter One

(Joshua 1:1) (Jasher 88:1)

Now after the death of Moses the servant of the LORD it came to pass, that the LORD spoke to Joshua the son of Nun, Moses' minister, saying,

(Joshua 1:2) (Jasher 88:2)

Moses my servant is dead; now therefore arise, go over this Jordan, you, and all this people, to the land which I do give to them, even to the children of Israel, and you shall make the children of Israel inherit the land.

(Joshua 1:3) (Jasher 88:3...)

Every place that the sole of your foot shall tread upon, that have I given to you, shall belong to you as I said to Moses.

(Joshua 1:4) (...Jasher 88:3)

From the wilderness and this Lebanon even to the great river of Perath, the river Euphrates, all the land of the Hittites, and to the great sea toward the going down of the sun, shall be your boundary coast.

(Joshua 1:5) (Jasher 88:4...)

There shall not any man be able to stand before you all the days of your life: as I was with Moses, so I will be with you: I will not fail you, nor forsake you.

(Joshua 1:6)

Be strong and of a good courage: for to this people shall you divide for an inheritance the land, which I swore to their fathers to give them.

(Joshua 1:7) (...Jasher 88:4)

Only be strong and very courageous, that you may observe to do according to all the law, which Moses my servant commanded you: turn not from it to the right hand or to the left, that you may prosper wherever you go, in all you do.

(Joshua 1:8)

This book of the law shall not depart out of your mouth; but you shall meditate therein day and night, that you may observe to do according to all that is written therein: for then you shall make your way prosperous, and then you shall have good success.

(Joshua 1:9)

Have not I commanded you? Be strong and of a good courage; be not afraid, neither be dismayed: for the LORD your God is with you wherever you go.

(Joshua 1:10) (Jasher 88:5...)

Then Joshua commanded the officers of the people of Israel, saying,

(Joshua 1:11) (...Jasher 88:5)

Pass through the host, and command the people, saying, Prepare for yourselves victuals; for within three days you shall pass over this Jordan, to go in to possess the land, which the LORD your God gives you to possess it.

(Joshua 1:12)

And to the Reubenites, and to the Gadites, and to half the

tribe of Manasseh, spoke Joshua, saying,

(Joshua 1:13)
Remember the word which Moses the servant of the LORD commanded you, saying, The LORD your God has given you rest, and has given you this land.

(Joshua 1:14)
Your wives, your little ones, and your cattle, shall remain in the land which Moses gave you on this side Jordan; but you shall pass before your brethren armed, all the mighty men of valor, and help them;

(Joshua 1:15)
Until the LORD have given your brethren rest, as he has given you, and they also have possessed the land which the LORD your God gives them: then you shall return to the land of your possession, and enjoy it, which Moses the LORD'S servant gave you on this side Jordan toward the sunrising.

(Joshua 1:16)
And they answered Joshua, saying, All that you command us we will do, and wherever you send us, we will go.

(Joshua 1:17)
According as we hearkened to Moses in all things, so will we hearken to you: only the LORD your God be with you, as he was with Moses.

(Joshua 1:18)
Whosoever rebels against your commandment, and will not hearken to your words in all that you command him, he shall be put to death: only be strong and of a good courage.

(Jasher 88:6)
And the officers of the children of Israel did so, and they commanded the people and they did all that Joshua had commanded.

Joshua: Chapter Two

(Joshua 2:1) (Jasher 88:7)

And Joshua the son of Nun sent out of Shittim two men to spy secretly out the land of Jericho, saying, Go view the land, even Jericho. And they went, and came into an harlot's house, named Rahab, and lodged there.

(Joshua 2:2)

And it was told the king of Jericho, saying, Behold, there came men in here tonight of the children of Israel to search out the country.

(Joshua 2:3)

And the king of Jericho sent to Rahab, saying, Bring forth the men that are come to you, which are entered into your house: for they be come to search out all the country.

(Joshua 2:4)

And the woman took the two men, and hid them, and said thus, There came men to me, but I wist not where they were:

(Joshua 2:5)

And it came to pass about the time of shutting of the gate, when it was dark, that the men went out: whither the men went I wot not: pursue after them quickly; for you shall overtake them.

(Joshua 2:6)

But she had brought them up to the roof of the house, and hid them with the stalks of flax, which she had laid in order upon the roof.

(Joshua 2:7)

And the men pursued after them the way to Jordan to the fords: and as soon as they which pursued after them were gone out, they shut the gate.

(Joshua 2:8)

And before they were laid down, she came up to them upon the roof;

(Joshua 2:9)

And she said to the men, I know that the LORD has given you the land, and that your terror is fallen upon us, and that all the inhabitants of the land faint because of you.

(Joshua 2:10)

For we have heard how the LORD dried up the water of the Red sea for you, when you came out of Egypt; and what you did to the two kings of the Amorites, that were on the other side Jordan, Sihon and Og, whom you utterly destroyed.

(Joshua 2:11)

And as soon as we had heard these things, our hearts melted, neither did there remain any more courage in any man, because of you: for the LORD your God, he is God in heaven above, and in earth beneath.

(Joshua 2:12)

Now therefore, I pray you, swear to me by the LORD, since I have shewed you kindness, that you will also shew kindness to my father's house, and give me a true token:

(Joshua 2:13)

And that you will save alive my father, and my mother, and my brethren, and my sisters, and all that they have, and deliver our lives from death.

(Joshua 2:14)

And the men answered her, Our life for yours, if you utter not this our business. And it shall be, when the LORD has given us the land, that we will deal kindly and truly with you.

(Joshua 2:15)

Then she let them down by a cord through the window: for her house was upon the town wall, and she dwelt upon the wall.

(Joshua 2:16)

And she said to them, Get you to the mountain, lest the pursuers meet you; and hide yourselves there three days, until the pursuers be returned: and afterward may you go your way.

(Joshua 2:17)

And the men said to her, We will be blameless of this your oath which you have made us swear.

(Joshua 2:18)

Behold, when we come into the land, you shall bind this line of scarlet thread in the window which let us down by: and you shall bring your father, and your mother, and your brethren, and all your father's household, home to you.

(Joshua 2:19)

And it shall be, that whosoever shall go out of the doors of your house into the street, his blood shall be upon his head, and we will be guiltless: and whosoever shall be with you in the house, his blood shall be on our head, if any hand be upon him.

(Joshua 2:20)

And if you utter this our business, then we will be quit of your oath which you have made us to swear.

(Joshua 2:21)

And she said, According to your words, so be it. And she sent them away, and they departed: and she bound the scarlet line in the window.

(Joshua 2:22)

And they went, and came to the mountain, and abode there three days, until the pursuers were returned: and the pursuers sought them throughout all the way, but found them not.

(Joshua 2:23) (Jasher 88:8...)

So at the end of seven days, the two men returned, and descended from the mountain, and passed over, and came to Joshua the son of Nun, in the camp and told him all things that befell them:

(Joshua 2:24) (...Jasher 88:8)

And they said to Joshua, Truly the LORD has delivered into our hands all the land; for even all the inhabitants of the country do faint with fear because of us.

Joshua: Chapter Three

(Joshua 3:1) (Jasher 88:9...)

And it came to pass that, Joshua rose early in the morning and all Israel with him; and they removed from Shittim, and came to Jordan, he and all the children of Israel, and lodged there before they passed over.

(Joshua 3:2)

And it came to pass after three days, that the officers went through the host;

(Joshua 3:3)

And they commanded the people, saying, When you see the ark of the covenant of the LORD your God, and the priests the Levites bearing it, then you shall remove from your place, and go after it.

(Joshua 3:4)

Yet there shall be a space between you and it, about two thousand cubits by measure: come not near to it, that you may know the way by which you must go: for you have not passed this way heretofore.

(Joshua 3:5)

And Joshua said to the people, Sanctify yourselves: for to morrow the LORD will do wonders among you.

(Joshua 3:6)

And Joshua spoke to the priests, saying, Take up the ark of the covenant, and pass over before the people. And they took up the ark of the covenant, and went before the people.

(Joshua 3:7)

And the LORD said to Joshua, This day will I begin to magnify you in the sight of all Israel, that they may know that, as I was with Moses, so I will be with you.

(Joshua 3:8)

And you shall command the priests that bear the ark of the covenant, saying, When you are come to the brink of the water of Jordan, you shall stand still in Jordan.

(Joshua 3:9)

And Joshua said to the children of Israel, Come here, and hear the words of the LORD your God.

(Joshua 3:10)

And Joshua said, Hereby you shall know that the living God is among you, and that he will without fail drive out from before you the Canaanites, and the Hittites, and the Hivites, and the Perizzites, and the Girgashites, and the Amorites, and the Jebusites.

(Joshua 3:11)

Behold, the ark of the covenant of the Lord of all the earth passes over before you into Jordan.

(Joshua 3:12)

Now therefore take you twelve men out of the tribes of Israel, out of every tribe a man.

(Joshua 3:13)

And it shall come to pass, as soon as the soles of the feet of the priests that bear the ark of the LORD, the Lord of all the earth, shall rest in the waters of Jordan, that the waters of Jordan shall be cut off from the waters that come down from above; and they shall stand upon an heap.

(Joshua 3:14)

And it came to pass, when the people removed from their tents, to pass over Jordan, and the priests bearing the ark of the covenant before the people;

(Joshua 3:15)

And as they that bare the ark were come to Jordan, and the feet of the priests that bare the ark were dipped in the brim of the water, (for Jordan overflows all his banks all the time of harvest,)

(Joshua 3:16)

That the waters which came down from above stood and rose up upon an heap very far from the city Adam, that is beside Zaretan: and those that came down toward the sea of the plain, even the salt sea, failed, and were cut off: and the people passed over right against Jericho.

(Joshua 3:17)

And the priests that bare the ark of the covenant of the LORD stood firm on dry ground in the midst of Jordan, and all the Israelites passed over on dry ground, until all the people were passed clean over Jordan.

Joshua: Chapter Four

(Joshua 4:1)
And it came to pass, when all the people were clean passed over Jordan, that the LORD spoke to Joshua, saying,

(Joshua 4:2)
Take you twelve men out of the people, out of every tribe a man,

(Joshua 4:3)
And command you them, saying, Take you hence out of the midst of Jordan, out of the place where the priests' feet stood firm, twelve stones, and you shall carry them over with you, and leave them in the lodging place, where you shall lodge this night.

(Joshua 4:4)
Then Joshua called the twelve men, whom he had prepared of the children of Israel, out of every tribe a man:

(Joshua 4:5)
And Joshua said to them, Pass over before the ark of the LORD your God into the midst of Jordan, and take up every man of you a stone upon his shoulder, according to the number of the tribes of the children of Israel:

(Joshua 4:6)
That this may be a sign among you, that when your children ask their fathers in time to come, saying, What mean you by these stones?

(Joshua 4:7)

Then you shall answer them, That the waters of Jordan were cut off before the ark of the covenant of the LORD; when it passed over Jordan, the waters of Jordan were cut off: and these stones shall be for a memorial to the children of Israel for ever.

(Joshua 4:8)

And the children of Israel did so as Joshua commanded, and took up twelve stones out of the midst of Jordan, as the LORD spoke to Joshua, according to the number of the tribes of the children of Israel, and carried them over with them to the place where they lodged, and laid them down there.

(Joshua 4:9)

And Joshua set up twelve stones in the midst of Jordan, in the place where the feet of the priests which bare the ark of the covenant stood: and they are there to this day.

(Joshua 4:10)

For the priests which bare the ark stood in the midst of Jordan, until every thing was finished that the LORD commanded Joshua to speak to the people, according to all that Moses commanded Joshua: and the people hasted and passed over.

(Joshua 4:11)

And it came to pass, when all the people were clean passed over, that the ark of the LORD passed over, and the priests, in the presence of the people.

(Joshua 4:12)

And the children of Reuben, and the children of Gad, and half the tribe of Manasseh, passed over armed before the children of Israel, as Moses spoke to them:

(Joshua 4:13)
About forty thousand prepared for war passed over before the LORD to battle, to the plains of Jericho.

(Joshua 4:14)
On that day the LORD magnified Joshua in the sight of all Israel; and they feared him, as they feared Moses, all the days of his life.

(Joshua 4:15)
And the LORD spoke to Joshua, saying,

(Joshua 4:16)
Command the priests that bear the ark of the testimony, that they come up out of Jordan.

(Joshua 4:17)
Joshua therefore commanded the priests, saying, Come you up out of Jordan.

(Joshua 4:18)
And it came to pass, when the priests that bare the ark of the covenant of the LORD were come up out of the midst of Jordan, and the soles of the priests' feet were lifted up to the dry land, that the waters of Jordan returned to their place, and flowed over all his banks, as they did before.

(...Jasher 88:9)
And Joshua and all Israel with him passed the Jordan; and Joshua was eighty-two years old when he passed the Jordan with Israel.

(Joshua 4:19) (Jasher 88:10)
And the people came up out of Jordan on the tenth day of

the first month, and encamped in Gilgal, in the east border of Jericho.

(Joshua 4:20)
And those twelve stones, which they took out of Jordan, did Joshua pitch in Gilgal.

(Joshua 4:21)
And he spoke to the children of Israel, saying, When your children shall ask their fathers in time to come, saying, What mean these stones?

(Joshua 4:22)
Then you shall let your children know, saying, Israel came over this Jordan on dry land.

(Joshua 4:23)
For the LORD your God dried up the waters of Jordan from before you, until you were passed over, as the LORD your God did to the Red sea, which he dried up from before us, until we were gone over:

(Joshua 4:24)
That all the people of the earth might know the hand of the LORD, that it is mighty: that you might fear the LORD your God for ever.

Joshua: Chapter Five

(Joshua 5:1)

And it came to pass, when all the kings of the Amorites, which were on the side of Jordan westward, and all the kings of the Canaanites, which were by the sea, heard that the LORD had dried up the waters of Jordan from before the children of Israel, until we were passed over, that their heart melted, neither was there spirit in them any more, because of the children of Israel.

(Joshua 5:2)

At that time the LORD said to Joshua, Make sharp knives, and circumcise again the children of Israel the second time.

(Joshua 5:3)

And Joshua made him sharp knives, and circumcised the children of Israel at the hill of the foreskins.

(Joshua 5:4)

And this is the cause why Joshua did circumcise: All the people that came out of Egypt, that were males, even all the men of war, died in the wilderness by the way, after they came out of Egypt.

(Joshua 5:5)

Now all the people that came out were circumcised: but all the people that were born in the wilderness by the way as they came forth out of Egypt, them they had not circumcised.

(Joshua 5:6)

For the children of Israel walked forty years in the wilderness, till all the people that were men of war, which came out of Egypt, were consumed, because they obeyed not the voice of the LORD: to whom the LORD swore that he would not shew them the land, which the LORD swore to their fathers that he would give us, a land that flows with milk and honey.

(Joshua 5:7)

And their children, whom he raised up in their stead, them Joshua circumcised: for they were uncircumcised, because they had not circumcised them by the way.

(Joshua 5:8)

And it came to pass, when they had done circumcising all the people, that they abode in their places in the camp, till they were whole.

(Joshua 5:9)

And the LORD said to Joshua, This day have I rolled away the reproach of Egypt from off you. Why the name of the place is called Gilgal to this day.

(Joshua 5:10) (Jasher 88:11)

And the children of Israel encamped in Gilgal, and kept the passover, as it is written in the law of Moses, on the fourteenth day of the month at even in the plains of Jericho.

(Joshua 5:11)

And they did eat of the old corn of the land on the morrow after the passover, unleavened cakes, and parched corn in the selfsame day.

(Joshua 5:12) (Jasher 88:12)

And the manna ceased at that time on the morrow of the Passover, after they had eaten of the old corn of the land; neither had the children of Israel manna any more; but they ate of the fruit of the land of Canaan that year.

(Joshua 5:13)

And it came to pass, when Joshua was by Jericho, that he lifted up his eyes and looked, and, behold, there stood a man over against him with his sword drawn in his hand: and Joshua went to him, and said to him, Are You for us, or for our adversaries?

(Joshua 5:14)

And he said, Nay; but as captain of the host of the LORD am I now come. And Joshua fell on his face to the earth, and did worship, and said to him, What saith my lord to his servant?

(Joshua 5:15)

And the captain of the LORD'S host said to Joshua, Loose your shoe from off your foot; for the place whereon you stand is holy. And Joshua did so.

Joshua: Chapter Six

(Joshua 6:1) (Jasher 88:13)

Now Jericho was straitly shut up because of the children of Israel: none went out, and none came in.

(Joshua 6:2) (Jasher 88:14...)

And it was in the second month, on the first day of the month, that the LORD said to Joshua, Rise up, See, I have given into your hand Jericho, and the king thereof, and the mighty men of valor, and all the people thereof.

(Joshua 6:3) (...Jasher 88:14)

And you shall compass the city, all you men of war, and go round about the city once each day. Thus shall you do six days.

(Joshua 6:4)

And seven priests shall bear before the ark seven trumpets of rams' horns: and the seventh day you shall compass the city seven times, and the priests shall blow with the trumpets.

(Joshua 6:5) (Jasher 88:15)

And it shall come to pass, that when the priests shall blow upon trumpets, they make a long blast with the ram's horn, and when you hear the sound of the trumpet, all the people shall shout with a great shout; and the wall of the city shall fall down flat, and the people shall ascend up every man straight before him. All the people shall go up every man against his opponent.

(Jasher 88:16)
And Joshua did so according to all that the Lord had commanded him.

(Joshua 6:6)
And Joshua the son of Nun called the priests, and said to them, Take up the ark of the covenant, and let seven priests bear seven trumpets of rams' horns before the ark of the LORD.

(Joshua 6:7)
And he said to the people, Pass on, and compass the city, and let him that is armed pass on before the ark of the LORD.

(Joshua 6:8)
And it came to pass, when Joshua had spoken to the people, that the seven priests bearing the seven trumpets of rams' horns passed on before the LORD, and blew with the trumpets: and the ark of the covenant of the LORD followed them.

(Joshua 6:9)
And the armed men went before the priests that blew with the trumpets, and the rearward came after the ark, the priests going on, and blowing with the trumpets.

(Joshua 6:10)
And Joshua had commanded the people, saying, You shall not shout, nor make any noise with your voice, neither shall any word proceed out of your mouth, until the day I bid you shout; then shall you shout.

(Joshua 6:11)
So the ark of the LORD compassed the city, going about it once: and they came into the camp, and lodged in the camp.

(Joshua 6:12)

And Joshua rose early in the morning, and the priests took up the ark of the LORD.

(Joshua 6:13)

And seven priests bearing seven trumpets of rams' horns before the ark of the LORD went on continually, and blew with the trumpets: and the armed men went before them; but the rearward came after the ark of the LORD, the priests going on, and blowing with the trumpets.

(Joshua 6:14)

And the second day they compassed the city once, and returned into the camp: so they did six days.

(Joshua 6:15) (Jasher 88:17...)

And it came to pass on the seventh day, that they rose early about the dawning of the day, and compassed the city after the same manner seven times: only on that day they compassed the city seven times.

(Joshua 6:16) (...Jasher 88:17, 18)

And it came to pass at the seventh time around, when the priests blew with the trumpets, Joshua said to the people, Shout; for the LORD has given you the whole city into your hands.

(Joshua 6:17) (Jasher 88:19...)

And only the city shall be accursed, even it, and all that are therein, and all it contains, to the LORD: only Rahab the harlot shall live, she and all that are with her in the house, because she hid the messengers that we sent.

(Joshua 6:18) (...Jasher 88:19)

And you, in any wise keep yourselves from the accursed thing, lest you make yourselves accursed, when you take of the accursed thing, and make the camp of Israel a curse, and trouble it.

(Joshua 6:19) (Jasher 88:20)

But all the silver, and gold, and vessels of brass and iron, are consecrated to the LORD: they shall come into the treasury of the LORD.

(Joshua 6:20) (Jasher 88:21...)

So the people shouted when the priests blew with the trumpets: and it came to pass, when the people heard the sound of the trumpet, and the people shouted with a great shout, that the wall of Jerico fell down flat, so that the people went up into the city, every man straight before him, and they took the city.

(Joshua 6:21) (...Jasher 88:21)

And they utterly destroyed all that was in the city, both man and woman, young and old, and ox, and sheep, and donkey, with the edge of the sword.

(Joshua 6:22)

But Joshua had said to the two men that had spied out the country, Go into the harlot's house, and bring out there the woman, and all that she has, as you swore to her.

(Joshua 6:23)

And the young men that were spies went in, and brought out Rahab, and her father, and her mother, and her brethren, and all that she had; and they brought out all her kindred, and left them without the camp of Israel.

(Joshua 6:24) (Jasher 88:22)

And they burnt the city with fire, and all that was therein: only the silver, and the gold, and the vessels of brass and of iron, they put into the treasury of the house of the LORD.

(Joshua 6:25)

And Joshua saved Rahab the harlot alive, and her father's household, and all that she had; and she dwells in Israel even to this day; because she hid the messengers, which Joshua sent to spy out Jericho.

(Joshua 6:26) (Jasher 88:23)

And Joshua adjured them and swore at that time, saying, Cursed be the man before the LORD, that rises up and builds this city Jericho: he shall lay the foundation thereof in his firstborn, and in his youngest son shall he set up the gates of it.

(Joshua 6:27)

So the LORD was with Joshua; and his fame was noised throughout all the country.

(Joshua 7:1) (Jasher 88:24)

But the children of Israel committed a trespass in the accursed thing: for Achan, the son of Carmi, the son of Zabdi, the son of Zerah, of the tribe of Judah, dealt treacherously in the accursed thing, and he took of the accursed thing and hid it in his tent: and the anger of the LORD was kindled against the children of Israel.

(Joshua 7:2) (Jasher 88:25, 26...)

And it was after this when the children of Israel had returned from burning Jericho, Joshua sent men from Jericho to spy out, and to fight against, also Ai, which is beside Bethaven, on the east side of Bethel, and spoke to them, saying, Go up and view the country. And the men went up and viewed Ai.

(Joshua 7:3) (...Jasher 88:26)

And they returned to Joshua, and said to him, Let not all the people go up to Ai; but let about two or three thousand men go up and smite the city, Ai; and make not all the people to labor there; for they are but few.

(Joshua 7:4) (Jasher 88:27, 28...)

So Joshua did so, and there went up there with him of the people of Israel about three thousand men: and they fought against the men of Ai. And the battle was severe against Israel, and the children of Israel fled before the men of Ai.

(Joshua 7:5) (...Jasher 88:28)

And the men of Ai smote of them about thirty and six men

of Israel: for they chased them from before the gate even to Shebarim, and smote them in the going down: why the hearts of the people melted, and became as water.

(Joshua 7:6) (Jasher 88:29)
And when Joshua saw this thing, he rent his clothes, and fell to the earth upon his face before the ark of the LORD until the eventide, he and the elders of Israel, and put dust upon their heads.

(Joshua 7:7) (Jasher 88:30...)
And Joshua said, Alas, O Lord GOD, why have you at all brought this people over the Jordan, to deliver us into the hand of the Amorites, to destroy us? Would to God we had been content, and dwelt on the other side Jordan!

(Joshua 7:8) (...Jasher 88:30)
O Lord, what shall I say, when Israel turns their backs before their enemies!

(Joshua 7:9) (Jasher 88:31)
For now therefore all the Canaanites and all the inhabitants of the land shall hear of it, and shall environ us round, and cut off our name from the earth: and what will you do to your great name?

(Joshua 7:10) (Jasher 88:32...)
And the LORD said to Joshua, Rise and get up; why lie thus upon your face?

(Joshua 7:11) (...Jasher 88:32)
For Israel has sinned, and they have also transgressed my covenant which I commanded them: for they have even taken of the accursed thing, and have also stolen, and dissembled

also, and they have put it even among their own stuff.

(Joshua 7:12)

Therefore the children of Israel could not stand before their enemies, but turned their backs before their enemies, because they were accursed: neither will I be with you any more, except you destroy the accursed from among you.

(Joshua 7:13)

Up, sanctify the people, and say, Sanctify yourselves against to morrow: for thus saith the LORD God of Israel, There is an accursed thing in the midst of you, O Israel: You can not stand before your enemies, until you take away the accursed thing from among you.

(Joshua 7:14)

In the morning therefore you shall be brought according to your tribes: and it shall be, that the tribe which the LORD takes shall come according to the families thereof; and the family which the LORD shall take shall come by households; and the household which the LORD shall take shall come man by man.

(Joshua 7:15)

And it shall be, that he that is taken with the accursed thing shall be burnt with fire, he and all that he has: because he has transgressed the covenant of the LORD, and because he has wrought folly in Israel.

(Joshua 7:16) (Jasher 88:33...)

So Joshua rose up early in the morning, and assembled the people, and brought the Urim by the order of the Lord, and brought Israel by their tribes; and the tribe of Judah was taken:

(Joshua 7:17)

And he brought the family of Judah; and he took the family of the Zarhites: and he brought the family of the Zarhites man by man; and Zabdi was taken:

(Joshua 7:18) (...Jasher 88:33)

And he brought his household man by man; and Achan, the son of Carmi, the son of Zabdi, the son of Zerah, of the tribe of Judah, was taken.

(Joshua 7:19) (Jasher 88:34...)

And Joshua said to Achan, My son, give, I pray you, glory to the LORD God of Israel, and make confession to him; and tell me now what you have done; hide it not from me.

(Joshua 7:20) (...Jasher 88:34...)

And Achan answered Joshua, and said, Indeed I have sinned against the LORD God of Israel, and thus and thus have I done:

(Joshua 7:21) (...Jasher 88:34)

When I saw among the spoils a goodly Babylonish garment of Shinar, and two hundred shekels of silver, and a wedge of gold of fifty shekels weight, then I coveted them, and took them; and, behold, they are hid in the earth in the midst of my tent, and the silver under it.

(Joshua 7:22) (Jasher 88:35...)

So Joshua sent messengers, and they went and ran to the tent; and, behold, it was hid in his tent, and the silver under it.

(Joshua 7:23) (...Jasher 88:35)

And they took them out of the midst of the tent of Achan, and brought them to Joshua, and to all the children of Israel, and laid them out before the LORD.

(Joshua 7:24) (Jasher 88:36)

And Joshua, and all Israel with him, took Achan the son of Zerah, and the silver, and the garment, and the wedge of gold - all these utensils, and his sons, and his daughters, and his oxen, and his donkeys, and his sheep, and his tent, and all that he had: and they brought them to the valley of Achor.

(Joshua 7:25) (Jasher 88:37...)

And Joshua said, Why have you troubled us? The LORD shall trouble you this day. And all Israel stoned him with stones, and burned them there with fire, after they had stoned them with stones.

(Joshua 7:26) (...Jasher 88:37...)

And they raised over him a great heap of stones to this day. So the LORD's anger was appeased and he turned from the fierceness of his anger. Why the name of that place was called, The valley of Achor, to this day.

Joshua: Chapter Eight

(Jasher ...88:37)
And Joshua afterward came to the city and fought against it.

(Joshua 8:1) (Jasher 88:38...)
And the LORD said to Joshua, Fear not, neither be dismayed: take all the people of war with you, and arise, go up to Ai: see, I have given into your hand the king of Ai, and his people, and his city, and his land:

(Joshua 8:2) (...Jasher 88:38)
And you shall do to them, Ai and her king, as you did to Jericho and her king: only the spoil thereof, and the cattle thereof, shall you take for a prey to yourselves: lay you an ambush for the city behind it.

(Joshua 8:3) (Jasher 88:39...)
So Joshua did according to the word of the Lord. He arose, and all the people of war, to go up against Ai: and Joshua chose out from among the sons of war thirty thousand mighty men of valor, and sent them away by night.

(Joshua 8:4) (Jasher 88:40...)
And he commanded them, saying, Behold, you shall lie in wait against the city, even behind the city: go not very far from the city, but be you all ready:

(Joshua 8:5) (...Jasher 88:40...)
And when you shall see us, I, and all the people that are with me, will approach to the city: and it shall come to pass, when

they come out against us, as at the first, that we will flee before them with cunning,

(Joshua 8:6) (...Jasher 88:40...)

(For they will come out after us) till we have drawn them from the city; for they will say, They flee before us, as at the first: therefore we will flee before them.

(Joshua 8:7)

Then you shall rise up from the ambush, and seize upon the city: for the LORD your God will deliver it into your hand.

(Joshua 8:8) (...Jasher 88:40)

And it shall be, when you have taken the city, that you shall set the city on fire: according to the commandment of the LORD shall you do. See, I have commanded you. And they did so.

(Joshua 8:9) (...Jasher 88:39)

Joshua therefore sent them forth: and they went to lie in ambush for the city, and abode between Bethel and Ai, on the west side of Ai: but Joshua lodged that night among the people.

(Joshua 8:10)

And Joshua rose up early in the morning, and numbered the people, and went up, he and the elders of Israel, before the people to Ai.

(Joshua 8:11)

And all the people, even the people of war that were with him, went up, and drew nigh, and came before the city, and pitched on the north side of Ai: now there was a valley between them and Ai.

(Joshua 8:12)

And he took about five thousand men, and set them to lie in ambush between Bethel and Ai, on the west side of the city.

(Joshua 8:13)

And when they had set the people, even all the host that was on the north of the city, and those lying in wait on the west of the city, Joshua went that night into the midst of the valley.

(Joshua 8:14) (Jasher 88:41)

And it came to pass, when the king of Ai saw it, that they hasted and rose up early. And Joshua fought, and the men of the city went out against Israel to battle, he and all his people, at a time appointed, before the plain; but he knew not that there were some lying in ambush against him behind the city.

(Joshua 8:15) (Jasher 88:42)

And Joshua and all Israel feigned themselves wearied out before them and made as if they were beaten before them, and fled by the way of the wilderness with cunning.

(Joshua 8:16) (Jasher 88:43...)

And all the people that were in Ai were called together to pursue after them: and they went out and they pursued after Joshua, and were drawn away from the city.

(Joshua 8:17) (...Jasher 88:43)

And there was not a man left in Ai or Bethel, that went not out after Israel: and they left the city open, and pursued after Israel.

(Joshua 8:18)

And the LORD said to Joshua, Stretch out the spear that is in your hand toward Ai; for I will give it into your hand. And

Joshua stretched out the spear that he had in his hand toward the city.

(Joshua 8:19) (Jasher 88:44...)
And those who were lying in ambush arose quickly out of their place, and they ran and hastened to come to the city as soon as he had stretched out his hand: and they entered into the city, and took it, and hasted and set the city on fire.

(Joshua 8:20) (...Jasher 88:44)
And when the men of Ai looked behind them, they saw, and, behold, the smoke of the city ascended up to heaven, and they had no power to flee this way or that way: and the people that fled to the wilderness turned back upon the pursuers.

(Joshua 8:21)
And when Joshua and all Israel saw that the ambush had taken the city, and that the smoke of the city ascended, then they turned again, and slew the men of Ai.

(Joshua 8:22) (Jasher 88:45)
And the other issued out of the city against them; so they, all the men of Ai, were in the midst of Israel, some on this side, and some on that side: and they smote them, so that they let none of them remain or escape.

(Joshua 8:23) (Jasher 88:46...)
And the children of Israel took Melosh the king of Ai alive, and brought him to Joshua.

(Joshua 8:24) (Jasher 88:47)
And it came to pass, when Israel had made an end of slaying all the inhabitants of Ai in the field, in the wilderness wherein they chased them, and when they were all fallen on the edge

of the sword, until they were consumed, that all the Israelites returned to Ai after having burned it, and they smote all those that were in it with the edge of the sword.

(Joshua 8:25) (Jasher 88:48...)

And so it was, that the number of all that fell that day, both of men and women, were twelve thousand, even all of the men of Ai.

(Joshua 8:26)

For Joshua drew not his hand back, wherewith he stretched out the spear, until he had utterly destroyed all the inhabitants of Ai.

(Joshua 8:27) (...Jasher 88:48)

Only the cattle and the spoil of that city Israel took for a prey to themselves, according to the word of the LORD which he commanded to Joshua.

(Joshua 8:28)

And Joshua burnt Ai, and made it an heap for ever, even a desolation to this day.

(Joshua 8:29) (...Jasher 88:46)

And the king of Ai, Joshua hanged on a tree until eventide and he died: and as soon as the sun was down, Joshua commanded that they should take his carcase down from the tree, and cast it at the entering of the gate of the city, and raise thereon a great heap of stones, that remains to this day.

(Joshua 8:30)

Then Joshua built an altar to the LORD God of Israel in mount Ebal,

(Joshua 8:31)

As Moses the servant of the LORD commanded the children of Israel, as it is written in the book of the law of Moses, an altar of whole stones, over which no man has lift up any iron: and they offered thereon burnt offerings to the LORD, and sacrificed peace offerings.

(Joshua 8:32)

And he wrote there upon the stones a copy of the law of Moses, which he wrote in the presence of the children of Israel.

(Joshua 8:33)

And all Israel, and their elders, and officers, and their judges, stood on this side the ark and on that side before the priests the Levites, which bare the ark of the covenant of the LORD, as well the stranger, as he that was born among them; half of them over against mount Gerizim, and half of them over against mount Ebal; as Moses the servant of the LORD had commanded before, that they should bless the people of Israel.

(Joshua 8:34)

And afterward he read all the words of the law, the blessings and cursings, according to all that is written in the book of the law.

(Joshua 8:35)

There was not a word of all that Moses commanded, which Joshua read not before all the congregation of Israel, with the women, and the little ones, and the strangers that were conversant among them.

Joshua: Chapter Nine

(Joshua 9:1) (Jasher 88:49...)

And it came to pass, when all the kings which were on this side Jordan, in the hills, and in the valleys, and in all the coasts of the great sea over against Lebanon, the Hittite, and the Amorite, the Canaanite, the Perizzite, the Hivite, and the Jebusite, all the kings of Canaan, heard thereof of the evil which the children of Israel had done to Jericho and to Ai.

(Joshua 9:2) (...Jasher 88:49)

That they gathered themselves together, to fight with Joshua and with Israel, with one accord.

(Joshua 9:3)

And the inhabitants of Gibeon heard what Joshua had done to Jericho and to Ai.

(Joshua 9:4) (Jasher 88:50...)

Only the inhabitants of Gibeon were greatly afraid of fighting against the Israelites lest they should perish, so they worked wilily, and acted cunningly, and went and made as if they had been ambassadors, and took old sacks upon their donkeys, and wine bottles, old, and rent, and bound up;

(Joshua 9:5)

And old shoes and clouted upon their feet, and old garments upon them; and all the bread of their provision was dry and moldy.

(Joshua 9:6) (...Jasher 88:50)

And they went to Joshua and to all Israel to the camp at Gilgal, and said to him and to the men of Israel, We be come from a far country: now therefore make a league with us.

(Joshua 9:7)

And the men of Israel said to the Hivites, Peradventure you dwell among us; and how shall we make a league with you?

(Joshua 9:8)

And they said to Joshua, We are your servants. And Joshua said to them, Who are you? And from whence come you?

(Joshua 9:9)

And they said to him, From a very far country your servants are come because of the name of the LORD your God: for we have heard the fame of him, and all that he did in Egypt,

(Joshua 9:10)

And all that he did to the two kings of the Amorites, that were beyond Jordan, to Sihon king of Heshbon, and to Og king of Bashan, which was at Ashtaroth.

(Joshua 9:11)

Why our elders and all the inhabitants of our country spoke to us, saying, Take victuals with you for the journey, and go to meet them, and say to them, We are your servants: therefore now make you a league with us.

(Joshua 9:12)

This our bread we took hot for our provision out of our houses on the day we came forth to go to you; but now, behold, it is dry, and it is moldy:

(Joshua 9:13)

And these bottles of wine, which we filled, were new; and, behold, they be rent: and these our garments and our shoes are become old by reason of the very long journey.

(Joshua 9:14)

And the men took of their victuals, and asked not counsel at the mouth of the LORD.

(Joshua 9:15) (Jasher 88:51...)

And the inhabitants of Gibeon over-reached the children of Israel, and the children of Israel and Joshua made peace with them, and made a league with them, to let them live: and the princes of the congregation swore to them.

(Joshua 9:16) (...Jasher 88:51)

And it came to pass afterwards, at the end of three days after they had made a league with them, that they heard that they were their neighbors, and that they dwelt among them.

(Joshua 9:17)

And the children of Israel journeyed, and came to their cities on the third day. Now their cities were Gibeon, and Chephirah, and Beeroth, and Kirjathjearim.

(Joshua 9:18) (Jasher 88:52...)

And the children of Israel smote them not, because the princes of the congregation had sworn to them by the LORD God of Israel. And all the congregation murmured against the princes.

(Joshua 9:19)

But all the princes said to all the congregation, We have sworn to them by the LORD God of Israel: now therefore we may not touch them.

(Joshua 9:20)
This we will do to them; we will even let them live, lest wrath be upon us, because of the oath which we swore to them.

(Joshua 9:21)
And the princes said to them, Let them live; but let them be hewers of wood and drawers of water to all the congregation; as the princes had promised them.

(Joshua 9:22) (Jasher 88:53...)
And Joshua called for them, and he spoke to them, saying, Why have you beguiled us, to do this thing to us? saying, We are very far from you; when you dwell among us?

(Joshua 9:23)
Now therefore you are cursed, and there shall none of you be freed from being bondmen, and hewers of wood and drawers of water for the house of my God.

(Joshua 9:24) (...Jasher 88:53)
And they answered Joshua, and said, Because it was certainly told to your servants, all that you had done to all the kings of the Amorites, how that the LORD your God commanded his servant Moses to give you all the land, and to destroy all the inhabitants of the land from before you, therefore we were sore afraid of our lives because of you, and have done this thing.

(Joshua 9:25)
And now, behold, we are in your hand: as it seems good and right to you to do to us, do.

(Joshua 9:26)

And so did he to them, and delivered them out of the hand of the children of Israel, that they slew them not.

(Joshua 9:27) (...Jasher 88:52, 54)

And Joshua made them that day hewers of wood and drawers of water for the congregation, and he divided them for slaves to all the tribes of Israel, and for the altar of the LORD, even to this day, in the place which he should choose.

Joshua: Chapter Ten

(Joshua 10:1) (Jasher 88:55...)

Now it came to pass, when Adonizedek king of Jerusalem had heard how Joshua had taken Ai, and had utterly destroyed it; as he had done to Jericho and her king, so he had done to Ai and her king; and how the inhabitants of Gibeon had made peace with Israel, and were among them;

(Joshua 10:2)

That they feared greatly, because Gibeon was a great city, as one of the royal cities, and because it was greater than Ai, and all the men thereof were mighty.

(Joshua 10:3) (...Jasher 88:55)

Why Adonizedek king of Jerusalem sent to Hoham king of Hebron, and to Piram king of Jarmuth, and to Japhia king of Lachish, and to Debir king of Eglon, saying,

(Joshua 10:4) (Jasher 88:56)

Come up to me, and help me, that we may smite the children of Israel and the inhabitants of Gibeon: for it has made peace with Joshua and with the children of Israel.

(Joshua 10:5...) (Jasher 88:57)

Therefore the five kings of the Amorites, the king of Jerusalem, the king of Hebron, the king of Jarmuth, the king of Lachish, the king of Eglon, they gathered themselves together, and five kings of the Amorites went up, they and all their hosts, a mighty people numerous as the sand of the sea shore,

(...Joshua 10:5) (Jasher 88:58...)

And all these kings came and encamped before Gibeon, and made war against it, and they began to fight against the inhabitants of Gibeon.

(Joshua 10:6) (...Jasher 88:58)

And all the men of Gibeon sent to Joshua to the camp to Gilgal, saying, Slack not your hand from your servants; come up to us quickly, and save us, and help us: for all the kings of the Amorites that dwell in the mountains are gathered together to fight against us.

(Joshua 10:7) (Jasher 88:59...)

So Joshua ascended from Gilgal, he, and all the people of war with him, and all the mighty men of valor.

(Joshua 10:8)

And the LORD said to Joshua, Fear them not: for I have delivered them into your hand; there shall not a man of them stand before you.

(Joshua 10:9) (...Jasher 88:59)

Joshua therefore came to them suddenly, and went up from Gilgal all night, and smote these five kings with a great slaughter.

(Joshua 10:10) (Jasher 88:60)

And the LORD discomfited them before the children of Israel, and slew them with a great slaughter at Gibeon, and chased them along the way that goes up to Bethhoron, and smote them to Azekah, and to Makkedah, and they fled from before the children of Israel.

(Joshua 10:11) (Jasher 88:61)

And it came to pass, as they fled from before Israel, and were in the going down to Bethhoron, that the LORD cast down great stones from heaven upon them to Azekah, and they died: they were more which died with hailstones than they whom the children of Israel slew with the sword.

(Jasher 88:62)

And the children of Israel pursued them, and they still smote them in the road, going on and smiting them.

(Joshua 10:12) (Jasher 88:63)

And when they were smiting, the day was declining toward evening. Then spoke Joshua to the LORD in the day when the LORD delivered up the Amorites before the children of Israel, and he said in the sight of Israel, Sun, stand still upon Gibeon; and Moon, in the valley of Ajalon.

(Joshua 10:13) (Jasher 88:64)

And the Lord hearkened to the voice of Joshua, and the sun stood still in the midst of the heavens, and it stood still six and thirty moments, and the moon also stayed and hastened not to go down a whole day, until the people had avenged themselves upon their enemies. Is not this written in the book of Jasher? So the sun stood still in the midst of heaven, and hasted not to go down about a whole day.

(Joshua 10:14) (Jasher 88:65)

And there was no day like that before it or after it, that the LORD hearkened to the voice of a man: for the LORD fought for Israel.

(Jasher 89:1)

Then spoke Joshua this song, on the day that the Lord had

given the Amorites into the hand of Joshua and the children of Israel, and he said in the sight of all Israel,

(Jasher 89:2)
You have done mighty things, O Lord, you have performed great deeds; who is like to you? My lips shall sing to your name.

(Jasher 89:3)
My goodness and my fortress, my high tower, I will sing a new song to you, with thanksgiving will I sing to you, you are the strength of my salvation.

(Jasher 89:4)
All the kings of the earth shall praise you, the princes of the world shall sing to you, the children of Israel shall rejoice in your salvation, they shall sing and praise your power.

(Jasher 89:5)
To you, O Lord, did we confide; we said you are our God, for you wast our shelter and strong tower against our enemies.

(Jasher 89:6)
To you we cried and were not ashamed, in you we trusted and were delivered; when we cried to you, you heard our voice, you did deliver our souls from the sword, you did show to us your grace, you did give to us your salvation, you did rejoice our hearts with your strength.

(Jasher 89:7)
You did go forth for our salvation, with your arm you did redeem your people; you did answer us from the heavens of your holiness, you did save us from ten thousands of people.

(Jasher 89:8)
The sun and moon stood still in heaven, and you did stand in your wrath against our oppressors and did command your judgments over them.

(Jasher 89:9)
All the princes of the earth stood up, the kings of the nations had gathered themselves together, they were not moved at your presence, they desired your battles.

(Jasher 89:10)
You did rise against them in your anger, and did bring down your wrath upon them; you did destroy them in your anger, and cut them off in your heart.

(Jasher 89:11)
Nations have been consumed with your fury, kingdoms have declined because of your wrath, you did wound kings in the day of your anger.

(Jasher 89:12)
You did pour out your fury upon them, your wrathful anger took hold of them; you did turn their iniquity upon them, and did cut them off in their wickedness.

(Jasher 89:13)
They did spread a trap, they fell therein, in the net they hid, their foot was caught.

(Jasher 89:14)
Your hand was ready for all your enemies who said, Through their sword they possessed the land, through their arm they dwelt in the city; you did fill their faces with shame, you did

bring their horns down to the ground, you did terrify them in your wrath, and did destroy them in your anger.

(Jasher 89:15)
The earth trembled and shook at the sound of your storm over them, you did not withhold their souls from death, and did bring down their lives to the grave.

(Jasher 89:16)
You did pursue them in your storm, you did consume them in your whirlwind, you did turn their rain into hail, they fell in deep pits so that they could not rise.

(Jasher 89:17)
Their carcasses were like rubbish cast out in the middle of the streets.

(Jasher 89:18)
They were consumed and destroyed in your anger, you did save your people with your might.

(Jasher 89:19)
Therefore our hearts rejoice in you, our souls exalt in your salvation.

(Jasher 89:20)
Our tongues shall relate your might, we will sing and praise your wondrous works.

(Jasher 89:21)
For you did save us from our enemies, you did deliver us from those who rose up against us, you did destroy them from before us and depress them beneath our feet.

(Jasher 89:22)
Thus shall all your enemies perish O Lord, and the wicked shall be like chaff driven by the wind, and your beloved shall be like trees planted by the waters.

(Joshua 10:15) (Jasher 89:23)
And Joshua returned, and all Israel with him, to the camp to Gilgal after having smitten all the kings, so that not a remnant was left of them.

(Joshua 10:16) (Jasher 89:24)
But these five kings fled alone on foot from battle, and hid themselves in a cave at Makkedah, and Joshua sought for them in the field of battle, and did not find them.

(Joshua 10:17) (Jasher 89:25)
And it was afterward told Joshua, saying, The five kings are behold they are found hid in a cave at Makkedah.

(Joshua 10:18) (Jasher 89:26)
And Joshua said, Roll great stones upon the mouth of the cave, and set men by it to keep them, lest they take themselves away; and the children of Israel did so.

(Joshua 10:19)
And stay you not, but pursue after your enemies, and smite the hindmost of them; suffer them not to enter into their cities: for the LORD your God has delivered them into your hand.

(Joshua 10:20)
And it came to pass, when Joshua and the children of Israel had made an end of slaying them with a very great slaughter,

till they were consumed, that the rest which remained of them entered into fenced cities.

(Joshua 10:21)

And all the people returned to the camp to Joshua at Makkedah in peace: none moved his tongue against any of the children of Israel.

(Joshua 10:22)

Then said Joshua, Open the mouth of the cave, and bring out those five kings to me out of the cave.

(Joshua 10:23)

And they did so, and brought forth those five kings to him out of the cave, the king of Jerusalem, the king of Hebron, the king of Jarmuth, the king of Lachish, and the king of Eglon.

(Joshua 10:24) (Jasher 89:27...)

And it came to pass, when they brought out those kings to Joshua, that Joshua called for all the men of Israel, and said to the captains of the men of war which went with him, Come near, put your feet upon the necks of these kings. And they came near, and put their feet upon the necks of them.

(Joshua 10:25) (...Jasher 89:27)

And Joshua said to them, Fear not, nor be dismayed, be strong and of good courage: for thus shall the LORD do to all your enemies against whom you fight.

(Joshua 10:26) (Jasher 89:28...)

And afterward Joshua commanded afterwards that they should smote them, and slew them, and hanged them on five trees: and they were hanging upon the trees until the evening.

(Joshua 10:27) (...Jasher 89:28)

And it came to pass at the time of the going down of the sun, that Joshua commanded, and they took them down off the trees, and cast them into the cave wherein they had been hid, and laid great stones in the cave's mouth, which remain until this very day.

(Joshua 10:28) (Jasher 89:29)

And that day Joshua went afterward with all the people that were with him to Makkedah, took Makkedah, and smote it with the edge of the sword, and the king thereof he utterly destroyed, them, and all the souls that were therein, and all belonging to the city; he let none remain: and he did to the king of Makkedah as he did to the king of Jericho.

(Joshua 10:29) (Jasher 89:30...)

Then Joshua passed from Makkedah, and all Israel with him, to Libnah, and fought against Libnah:

(Joshua 10:30) (...Jasher 89:31)

And the LORD delivered it also, and the king thereof, into the hand of Israel; and he smote it with the edge of the sword, and all the souls that were therein; he let none remain in it; but did to the king thereof as he did to the king of Jericho.

(Joshua 10:31) (Jasher 89:31...)

And Joshua passed from Libnah, and all Israel with him, to Lachish, and encamped against it, and fought against it:

(Joshua 10:32)

And the LORD delivered Lachish into the hand of Israel, which took it on the second day, and smote it with the edge of the sword, and all the souls that were therein, according to all that he had done to Libnah.

(Joshua 10:33) (...Jasher 89:32)
Then Horam king of Gezer came up to help the men of Lachish; and Joshua smote him and his people, until he had left him none remaining.

(Jasher 89:33)
And Joshua took Lachish and all the people thereof, and he did to it as he had done to Libnah.

(Joshua 10:34) (Jasher 89:34...)
And from Lachish Joshua passed to Eglon, and all Israel with him; and they encamped against it, and fought against it:

(Joshua 10:35) (...Jasher 89:34)
And they took it also on that day, and smote it and all the people thereof with the edge of the sword, and all the souls that were therein he utterly destroyed that day, according to all that he had done to Lachish.

(Joshua 10:36) (Jasher 89:35)
And Joshua went up from Eglon, and all Israel with him, to Hebron; and they fought against it:

(Joshua 10:37) (...Jasher 89:35...)
And they took it, and smote it with the edge of the sword, and the king thereof, and all the cities thereof, and all the souls that were therein; he left none remaining, according to all that he had done to Eglon; but destroyed it utterly, and all the souls that were therein.

(Joshua 10:38) (...Jasher 89:35...)
And Joshua returned from there, and all Israel with him, to Debir; and fought against it:

(Joshua 10:39) (...Jasher 89:35, 36)

And he took it, and the king thereof, and all the cities thereof; and they smote them with the edge of the sword, and utterly destroyed all the souls that were therein; he left none remaining: as he had done to Hebron, so he did to Debir, and to the king thereof as he had done to Jericho; as he had done also to Libnah, and to her king.

(Joshua 10:40) (Jasher 89:37...)

So Joshua smote all the country of the hills, and of the south, and of the vale, and of the springs, and all their kings of the Amorites: he left none remaining, but utterly destroyed all that breathed, as the LORD God of Israel commanded.

(Joshua 10:41) (...Jasher 89:37...)

And Joshua smote them from Kadeshbarnea even to Gaza, and all the country of Goshen, even to Gibeon.

(Joshua 10:42) (...Jasher 89:37)

And all these kings and their land did Joshua take at one time, because the LORD God of Israel fought for Israel.

(Joshua 10:43) (Jasher 89:38)

And Joshua returned, and all Israel with him, to the camp to Gilgal.

Joshua: Chapter Eleven

(Joshua 11:1) (Jasher 89:39...)

And it came to pass, when at that time Jabin king of Hazor had heard those things that Joshua had done to the kings of the Amorites, that he sent to Jobab king of Madon, and to the king of Shimron, and to the king of Achshaph.

(Joshua 11:2) (...Jasher 89:39...)

And to the kings of the Amorites that were on the north of the mountains, and of the plains south of Chinneroth, and in the valley, and in the borders of Dor on the west.

(Joshua 11:3)

And to the Canaanite on the east and on the west, and to the Amorite, and the Hittite, and the Perizzite, and the Jebusite in the mountains, and to the Hivite under Hermon in the land of Mizpeh.

(...Jasher 89:39, 40)

Saying, Come quickly to us and help us, that we may smite the children of Israel, before they come upon us and do to us as they have done to the other kings of the Amorites.

(Joshua 11:4) (Jasher 89:41)

And all these kings hearkened to the words of Jabin, king of Chazor, and they went out, they and all their hosts with them, seventeen kings, and their people were much people, even as numerous as the sand that is upon the sea shore in multitude, with horses and chariots very many.

(Joshua 11:5) (...Jasher 89:41)

And when all these kings were met together, they came and pitched together at the waters of Merom, and they were there together to fight against Israel.

(Joshua 11:6) (Jasher 89:42)

And the LORD said to Joshua, Be not afraid because of them: for to morrow about this time will I deliver them up all slain before Israel: You shall hough their horses, and burn their chariots with fire.

(Joshua 11:7) (Jasher 89:43...)

So Joshua came, and all the people of war with him, against them by the waters of Merom suddenly; and they fell upon them, and smote them, and they fell into their hands.

(Joshua 11:8) (...Jasher 89:43, 44)

And the LORD delivered them into the hand of the children of Israel, who smote them, and chased them to great Zidon, and to Misrephothmaim, and to the valley of Mizpeh eastward; So the children of Israel pursued all these kings with their camps, and they smote them, until they left them none remaining.

(Joshua 11:9)

And Joshua did to them as the LORD bade him: he houghed their horses, and burnt their chariots with fire.

(Joshua 11:10) (Jasher 89:45...)

And Joshua at that time turned back, and took Hazor, and smote the king thereof with the sword: for Hazor previously was the head of all those kingdoms.

(Joshua 11:11) (...Jasher 89:45...)

And they smote all the souls that were therein with the edge of the sword, utterly destroying them: there was not any left to breathe: and he burnt Hazor with fire.

(...Jasher 89:45)
And from Chazor, Joshua passed to Shimron and smote it and utterly destroyed it.

(Jasher 89:46)
From there he passed to Achshaph and he did to it as he had done to Shimron.

(Jasher 89:47)
From there he passed to Adulam and he smote all the people in it, and he did to Adulam as he had done to Achshaph and to Shimron.

(Joshua 11:12) (Jasher 89:48)
And he passed from them to all the cities of those kings, and all the kings of them did Joshua take, and smote them with the edge of the sword, and he smote all the people that were left of them and he utterly destroyed them, as Moses the servant of the LORD commanded.

(Joshua 11:13)
But as for the cities that stood still in their strength, Israel burned none of them, save Hazor only; that did Joshua burn.

(Joshua 11:14) (Jasher 89:49)
And all the spoil of these cities, and the cattle, the children of Israel took for a prey to themselves; but every man they smote with the edge of the sword, until they had destroyed them, neither left they any to breathe, they suffered not a soul to live.

(Joshua 11:15) (Jasher 89:50)

As the LORD commanded Moses his servant, so did Moses command Joshua, and so did Joshua and all Israel; he left nothing undone of all that the LORD commanded Moses, they failed not in anything.

(Joshua 11:16)

So Joshua took all that land, the hills, and all the south country, and all the land of Goshen, and the valley, and the plain, and the mountain of Israel, and the valley of the same;

(Joshua 11:17)

Even from the mount Halak, that goes up to Seir, even to Baalgad in the valley of Lebanon under mount Hermon: and all their kings he took, and smote them, and slew them.

(Joshua 11:18)

Joshua made war a long time with all those kings.

(Joshua 11:19)

There was not a city that made peace with the children of Israel, save the Hivites the inhabitants of Gibeon: all other they took in battle.

(Joshua 11:20)

For it was of the LORD to harden their hearts, that they should come against Israel in battle, that he might destroy them utterly, and that they might have no favor, but that he might destroy them, as the LORD commanded Moses.

(Joshua 11:21)

And at that time came Joshua, and cut off the Anakims from the mountains, from Hebron, from Debir, from Anab, and from all the mountains of Judah, and from all the mountains of Israel: Joshua destroyed them utterly with their cities.

(Joshua 11:22)

There was none of the Anakims left in the land of the children of Israel: only in Gaza, in Gath, and in Ashdod, there remained.

(Jasher 89:51)
So Joshua and all the children of Israel smote the whole land of Canaan as the Lord had commanded them, and smote all their kings, being thirty and one kings, and the children of Israel took their whole country.

(Jasher 89:52)
Besides the kingdoms of Sihon and Og which are on the other side Jordan, of which Moses had smitten many cities, and Moses gave them to the Reubenites and the Gadites and to half the tribe of Manasseh.

(Jasher 89:53)
And Joshua smote all the kings that were on this side Jordan to the west, and gave them for an inheritance to the nine tribes and to the half tribe of Israel.

(Jasher 89:54)
For five years, Joshua carried on the war with these kings, and he gave their cities to the Israelites, and the land became tranquil from battle throughout the cities of the Amorites and the Canaanites.

(Joshua 11:23)

So Joshua took the whole land, according to all that the LORD said to Moses; and Joshua gave it for an inheritance to Israel according to their divisions by their tribes. And the land rested from war.

Joshua: Chapter Twelve

(Joshua 12:1)

Now these are the kings of the land, which the children of Israel smote, and possessed their land on the other side Jordan toward the rising of the sun, from the river Arnon to mount Hermon, and all the plain on the east:

(Joshua 12:2)

Sihon king of the Amorites, who dwelt in Heshbon, and ruled from Aroer, which is upon the bank of the river Arnon, and from the middle of the river, and from half Gilead, even to the river Jabbok, which is the border of the children of Ammon;

(Joshua 12:3)

And from the plain to the sea of Chinneroth on the east, and to the sea of the plain, even the salt sea on the east, the way to Bethjeshimoth; and from the south, under Ashdothpisgah:

(Joshua 12:4)

And the coast of Og king of Bashan, which was of the remnant of the giants, that dwelt at Ashtaroth and at Edrei,

(Joshua 12:5)

And reigned in mount Hermon, and in Salcah, and in all Bashan, to the border of the Geshurites and the Maachathites, and half Gilead, the border of Sihon king of Heshbon.

(Joshua 12:6)

Them did Moses the servant of the LORD and the children of Israel smite: and Moses the servant of the LORD gave it for a possession to the Reubenites, and the Gadites, and the half tribe of Manasseh.

(Joshua 12:7)
And these are the kings of the country which Joshua and the children of Israel smote on this side Jordan on the west, from Baalgad in the valley of Lebanon even to the mount Halak, that goes up to Seir; which Joshua gave to the tribes of Israel for a possession according to their divisions;

(Joshua 12:8)
In the mountains, and in the valleys, and in the plains, and in the springs, and in the wilderness, and in the south country; the Hittites, the Amorites, and the Canaanites, the Perizzites, the Hivites, and the Jebusites:

(Joshua 12:9)
The king of Jericho, one; the king of Ai, which is beside Bethel, one;

(Joshua 12:10)
The king of Jerusalem, one; the king of Hebron, one;

(Joshua 12:11)
The king of Jarmuth, one; the king of Lachish, one;

(Joshua 12:12)
The king of Eglon, one; the king of Gezer, one;

(Joshua 12:13)
The king of Debir, one; the king of Geder, one;

(Joshua 12:14)
The king of Hormah, one; the king of Arad, one;

(Joshua 12:15)
The king of Libnah, one; the king of Adullam, one;

(Joshua 12:16)
The king of Makkedah, one; the king of Bethel, one;

(Joshua 12:17)
The king of Tappuah, one; the king of Hepher, one;

(Joshua 12:18)
The king of Aphek, one; the king of Lasharon, one;

(Joshua 12:19)
The king of Madon, one; the king of Hazor, one;

(Joshua 12:20)
The king of Shimronmeron, one; the king of Achshaph, one;

(Joshua 12:21)
The king of Taanach, one; the king of Megiddo, one;

(Joshua 12:22)
The king of Kedesh, one; the king of Jokneam of Carmel, one;

(Joshua 12:23)
The king of Dor in the coast of Dor, one; the king of the nations of Gilgal, one;

(Joshua 12:24) (...Jasher 89:51)
The king of Tirzah, one: all the kings thirty and one.

Joshua: Chapter Thirteen

(Jasher 90:1)
At that time in the fifth year after the children of Israel had passed over Jordan, after the children of Israel had rested from their war with the Canaanites, at that time great and severe battles arose between Edom and the children of Chittim, and the children of Chittim fought against Edom.

(Jasher 90:2)
And Abianus king of Chittim went forth in that year, that is in the thirty-first year of his reign, and a great force with him of the mighty men of the children of Chittim, and he went to Seir to fight against the children of Esau.

(Jasher 90:3)
And Hadad the king of Edom heard of his report, and he went forth to meet him with a heavy people and strong force, and engaged in battle with him in the field of Edom.

(Jasher 90:4)
And the hand of Chittim prevailed over the children of Esau, and the children of Chittim slew of the children of Esau, two and twenty thousand men, and all the children of Esau fled from before them.

(Jasher 90:5)
And the children of Chittim pursued them and they reached Hadad king of Edom, who was running before them and they caught him alive, and brought him to Abianus king of Chittim.

(Jasher 90:6)
And Abianus ordered him to be slain, and Hadad king of Edom died in the forty-eighth year of his reign.

(Jasher 90:7)
And the children of Chittim continued their pursuit of Edom, and they smote them with a great slaughter and Edom became subject to the children of Chittim.

(Jasher 90:8)
And the children of Chittim ruled over Edom, and Edom became under the hand of the children of Chittim and became one kingdom from that day.

(Jasher 90:9)
And from that time they could no more lift up their heads, and their kingdom became one with the children of Chittim.

(Jasher 90:10)
And Abianus placed officers in Edom and all the children of Edom became subject and tributary to Abianus, and Abianus turned back to his own land, Chittim.

(Jasher 90:11)
And when he returned he renewed his government and built for himself a spacious and fortified palace for a royal residence, and reigned securely over the children of Chittim and over Edom.

(Jasher 90:12)
In those days, after the children of Israel had driven away all the Canaanites and the Amorites, Joshua was old and advanced in years.

(Joshua 13:1) (Jasher 90:13)

Now Joshua was old and stricken in years; and the LORD said to him, You are old and stricken in years, and there remains yet very much land to be possessed.

(Joshua 13:2)

This is the land that yet remains: all the borders of the Philistines, and all Geshuri,

(Joshua 13:3)

From Sihor, which is before Egypt, even to the borders of Ekron northward, which is counted to the Canaanite: five lords of the Philistines; the Gazathites, and the Ashdothites, the Eshkalonites, the Gittites, and the Ekronites; also the Avites:

(Joshua 13:4)

From the south, all the land of the Canaanites, and Mearah that is beside the Sidonians, to Aphek, to the borders of the Amorites:

(Joshua 13:5)

And the land of the Giblites, and all Lebanon, toward the sunrising, from Baalgad under mount Hermon to the entering into Hamath.

(Joshua 13:6)

All the inhabitants of the hill country from Lebanon to Misrephothmaim, and all the Sidonians, them will I drive out from before the children of Israel: only divide it by lot to the Israelites for an inheritance, as I have commanded you.

(Joshua 13:7) (Jasher 90:14...)

Now therefore divide this land for an inheritance to the nine tribes, and the half tribe of Manasseh,

(Joshua 13:8)

With whom the Reubenites and the Gadites have received their inheritance, which Moses gave them, beyond Jordan eastward, even as Moses the servant of the LORD gave them;

(Joshua 13:9)

From Aroer, that is upon the bank of the river Arnon, and the city that is in the midst of the river, and all the plain of Medeba to Dibon;

(Joshua 13:10)

And all the cities of Sihon king of the Amorites, which reigned in Heshbon, to the border of the children of Ammon;

(Joshua 13:11)

And Gilead, and the border of the Geshurites and Maachathites, and all mount Hermon, and all Bashan to Salcah;

(Joshua 13:12)

All the kingdom of Og in Bashan, which reigned in Ashtaroth and in Edrei, who remained of the remnant of the giants: for these did Moses smite, and cast them out.

(Joshua 13:13)

Nevertheless the children of Israel expelled not the Geshurites, nor the Maachathites: but the Geshurites and the Maachathites dwell among the Israelites until this day.

(Joshua 13:14)

Only to the tribe of Levi he gave none inheritance; the sacrifices of the LORD God of Israel made by fire are their inheritance, as he said to them.

(Joshua 13:15)

And Moses gave to the tribe of the children of Reuben inheritance according to their families.

(Joshua 13:16)

And their coast was from Aroer, that is on the bank of the river Arnon, and the city that is in the midst of the river, and all the plain by Medeba;

(Joshua 13:17)

Heshbon, and all her cities that are in the plain; Dibon, and Bamothbaal, and Bethbaalmeon,

(Joshua 13:18)

And Jahazah, and Kedemoth, and Mephaath,

(Joshua 13:19)

And Kirjathaim, and Sibmah, and Zarethshahar in the mount of the valley,

(Joshua 13:20)

And Bethpeor, and Ashdothpisgah, and Bethjeshimoth,

(Joshua 13:21)

And all the cities of the plain, and all the kingdom of Sihon king of the Amorites, which reigned in Heshbon, whom Moses smote with the princes of Midian, Evi, and Rekem, and Zur, and Hur, and Reba, which were dukes of Sihon, dwelling in the country.

(Joshua 13:22)

Balaam also the son of Beor, the soothsayer, did the children of Israel slay with the sword among them that were slain by them.

(Joshua 13:23)

And the border of the children of Reuben was Jordan, and the border thereof. This was the inheritance of the children of Reuben after their families, the cities and the villages thereof.

(Joshua 13:24)

And Moses gave inheritance to the tribe of Gad, even to the children of Gad according to their families.

(Joshua 13:25)

And their coast was Jazer, and all the cities of Gilead, and half the land of the children of Ammon, to Aroer that is before Rabbah;

(Joshua 13:26)

And from Heshbon to Ramathmizpeh, and Betonim; and from Mahanaim to the border of Debir;

(Joshua 13:27)

And in the valley, Betharam, and Bethnimrah, and Succoth, and Zaphon, the rest of the kingdom of Sihon king of Heshbon, Jordan and his border, even to the edge of the sea of Chinnereth on the other side Jordan eastward.

(Joshua 13:28)

This is the inheritance of the children of Gad after their families, the cities, and their villages.

(Joshua 13:29)

And Moses gave inheritance to the half tribe of Manasseh: and this was the possession of the half tribe of the children of Manasseh by their families.

(Joshua 13:30)

And their coast was from Mahanaim, all Bashan, all the kingdom of Og king of Bashan, and all the towns of Jair, which are in Bashan, threescore cities:

(Joshua 13:31)

And half Gilead, and Ashtaroth, and Edrei, cities of the kingdom of Og in Bashan, were pertaining to the children of Machir the son of Manasseh, even to the one half of the children of Machir by their families.

(Joshua 13:32)

These are the countries which Moses did distribute for inheritance in the plains of Moab, on the other side Jordan, by Jericho, eastward.

(Joshua 13:33)

But to the tribe of Levi Moses gave not any inheritance: the LORD God of Israel was their inheritance, as he said to them.

(...Jasher 90:14)

And Joshua rose up and did as the Lord had spoken to him.

(Jasher 90:15)

And he divided the whole land to the tribes of Israel as an inheritance according to their divisions.

(Jasher 90:16)

But to the tribe at Levi he gave no inheritance, the offerings of the Lord are their inheritance as the Lord had spoken of them by the hand of Moses.

Joshua: Chapter Fourteen

(Joshua 14:1)

And these are the countries which the children of Israel inherited in the land of Canaan, which Eleazar the priest, and Joshua the son of Nun, and the heads of the fathers of the tribes of the children of Israel, distributed for inheritance to them.

(Joshua 14:2)

By lot was their inheritance, as the LORD commanded by the hand of Moses, for the nine tribes, and for the half tribe.

(Joshua 14:3)

For Moses had given the inheritance of two tribes and an half tribe on the other side Jordan: but to the Levites he gave none inheritance among them.

(Joshua 14:4)

For the children of Joseph were two tribes, Manasseh and Ephraim: therefore they gave no part to the Levites in the land, save cities to dwell in, with their suburbs for their cattle and for their substance.

(Joshua 14:5)

As the LORD commanded Moses, so the children of Israel did, and they divided the land.

(Joshua 14:6)

Then the children of Judah came to Joshua in Gilgal: and Caleb the son of Jephunneh the Kenezite said to him, You know the thing that the LORD said to Moses the man of God concerning me and you in Kadeshbarnea.

(Joshua 14:7)

Forty years old was I when Moses the servant of the LORD sent me from Kadeshbarnea to espy out the land; and I brought him word again as it was in mine heart.

(Joshua 14:8)

Nevertheless my brethren that went up with me made the heart of the people melt: but I wholly followed the LORD my God.

(Joshua 14:9)

And Moses swore on that day, saying, Surely the land whereon your feet have trodden shall be your inheritance, and your children's for ever, because you have wholly followed the LORD my God.

(Joshua 14:10)

And now, behold, the LORD has kept me alive, as he said, these forty and five years, even since the LORD spoke this word to Moses, while the children of Israel wandered in the wilderness: and now, lo, I am this day fourscore and five years old.

(Joshua 14:11)

As yet I am as strong this day as I was in the day that Moses sent me: as my strength was then, even so is my strength now, for war, both to go out, and to come in.

(Joshua 14:12)

Now therefore give me this mountain, whereof the LORD spoke in that day; for you heard in that day how the Anakims were there, and that the cities were great and fenced: if so be the LORD will be with me, then I shall be able to drive them out, as the LORD said.

(Joshua 14:13) (Jasher 90:17)

And Joshua blessed him, and gave to Caleb the son of Jephunneh one portion above his brothers, as the Lord had spoken through Moses - Hebron for an inheritance.

(Joshua 14:14) (Jasher 90:18)

Hebron therefore became the inheritance of Caleb the son of Jephunneh the Kenezite and to his children to this day, because that he wholly followed the LORD God of Israel.

(Joshua 14:15)

And the name of Hebron before was Kirjatharba; which Arba was a great man among the Anakims. And the land had rest from war.

Joshua: Chapter Fifteen

(Joshua 15:1)

This then was the lot of the tribe of the children of Judah by their families; even to the border of Edom the wilderness of Zin southward was the uttermost part of the south coast.

(Joshua 15:2)

And their south border was from the shore of the salt sea, from the bay that looks southward:

(Joshua 15:3)

And it went out to the south side to Maalehacrabbim, and passed along to Zin, and ascended up on the south side to Kadeshbarnea, and passed along to Hezron, and went up to Adar, and fetched a compass to Karkaa:

(Joshua 15:4)

From there it passed toward Azmon, and went out to the river of Egypt; and the goings out of that coast were at the sea: this shall be your south coast.

(Joshua 15:5)

And the east border was the salt sea, even to the end of Jordan. And their border in the north quarter was from the bay of the sea at the uttermost part of Jordan:

(Joshua 15:6)

And the border went up to Bethhogla, and passed along by the north of Betharabah; and the border went up to the stone of Bohan the son of Reuben:

(Joshua 15:7)

And the border went up toward Debir from the valley of Achor, and so northward, looking toward Gilgal, that is before the going up to Adummim, which is on the south side of the river: and the border passed toward the waters of Enshemesh, and the goings out thereof were at Enrogel:

(Joshua 15:8)

And the border went up by the valley of the son of Hinnom to the south side of the Jebusite; the same is Jerusalem: and the border went up to the top of the mountain that lies before the valley of Hinnom westward, which is at the end of the valley of the giants northward:

(Joshua 15:9)

And the border was drawn from the top of the hill to the fountain of the water of Nephtoah, and went out to the cities of mount Ephron; and the border was drawn to Baalah, which is Kirjathjearim:

(Joshua 15:10)

And the border compassed from Baalah westward to mount Seir, and passed along to the side of mount Jearim, which is Chesalon, on the north side, and went down to Bethshemesh, and passed on to Timnah:

(Joshua 15:11)

And the border went out to the side of Ekron northward: and the border was drawn to Shicron, and passed along to mount Baalah, and went out to Jabneel; and the goings out of the border were at the sea.

(Joshua 15:12)

And the west border was to the great sea, and the coast

thereof. This is the coast of the children of Judah round about according to their families.

(Joshua 15:13)

And to Caleb the son of Jephunneh he gave a part among the children of Judah, according to the commandment of the LORD to Joshua, even the city of Arba the father of Anak, which city is Hebron.

(Joshua 15:14)

And Caleb drove there the three sons of Anak, Sheshai, and Ahiman, and Talmai, the children of Anak.

(Joshua 15:15)

And he went up there to the inhabitants of Debir: and the name of Debir before was Kirjathsepher.

(Joshua 15:16)

And Caleb said, He that smites Kirjathsepher, and takes it, to him will I give Achsah my daughter to wife.

(Joshua 15:17)

And Othniel the son of Kenaz, the brother of Caleb, took it: and he gave him Achsah his daughter to wife.

(Joshua 15:18)

And it came to pass, as she came to him, that she moved him to ask of her father a field: and she lighted off her donkey; and Caleb said to her, What do you want?

(Joshua 15:19)

Who answered, Give me a blessing; for you have given me a south land; give me also springs of water. And he gave her the upper springs, and the nether springs.

(Joshua 15:20)
This is the inheritance of the tribe of the children of Judah according to their families.

(Joshua 15:21)
And the uttermost cities of the tribe of the children of Judah toward the coast of Edom southward were Kabzeel, and Eder, and Jagur,

(Joshua 15:22)
And Kinah, and Dimonah, and Adadah,

(Joshua 15:23)
And Kedesh, and Hazor, and Ithnan,

(Joshua 15:24)
Ziph, and Telem, and Bealoth,

(Joshua 15:25)
And Hazor, Hadattah, and Kerioth, and Hezron, which is Hazor,

(Joshua 15:26)
Amam, and Shema, and Moladah,

(Joshua 15:27)
And Hazargaddah, and Heshmon, and Bethpalet,

(Joshua 15:28)
And Hazarshual, and Beersheba, and Bizjothjah,

(Joshua 15:29)
Baalah, and Iim, and Azem,

(Joshua 15:30)
And Eltolad, and Chesil, and Hormah,

(Joshua 15:31)
And Ziklag, and Madmannah, and Sansannah,

(Joshua 15:32)
And Lebaoth, and Shilhim, and Ain, and Rimmon: all the cities are twenty and nine, with their villages:

(Joshua 15:33)
And in the valley, Eshtaol, and Zoreah, and Ashnah,

(Joshua 15:34)
And Zanoah, and Engannim, Tappuah, and Enam,

(Joshua 15:35)
Jarmuth, and Adullam, Socoh, and Azekah,

(Joshua 15:36)
And Sharaim, and Adithaim, and Gederah, and Gederothaim; fourteen cities with their villages:

(Joshua 15:37)
Zenan, and Hadashah, and Migdalgad,

(Joshua 15:38)
And Dilean, and Mizpeh, and Joktheel,

(Joshua 15:39)
Lachish, and Bozkath, and Eglon,

(Joshua 15:40)
And Cabbon, and Lahmam, and Kithlish,

(Joshua 15:41)
And Gederoth, Bethdagon, and Naamah, and Makkedah; sixteen cities with their villages:

(Joshua 15:42)
Libnah, and Ether, and Ashan,

(Joshua 15:43)
And Jiphtah, and Ashnah, and Nezib,

(Joshua 15:44)
And Keilah, and Achzib, and Mareshah; nine cities with their villages:

(Joshua 15:45)
Ekron, with her towns and her villages:

(Joshua 15:46)
From Ekron even to the sea, all that lay near Ashdod, with their villages:

(Joshua 15:47)
Ashdod with her towns and her villages, Gaza with her towns and her villages, to the river of Egypt, and the great sea, and the border thereof:

(Joshua 15:48)
And in the mountains, Shamir, and Jattir, and Socoh,

(Joshua 15:49)
And Dannah, and Kirjathsannah, which is Debir,

(Joshua 15:50)
And Anab, and Eshtemoh, and Anim,

(Joshua 15:51)
And Goshen, and Holon, and Giloh; eleven cities with their villages:

(Joshua 15:52)
Arab, and Dumah, and Eshean,

(Joshua 15:53)
And Janum, and Bethtappuah, and Aphekah,

(Joshua 15:54)
And Humtah, and Kirjatharba, which is Hebron, and Zior; nine cities with their villages:

(Joshua 15:55)
Maon, Carmel, and Ziph, and Juttah,

(Joshua 15:56)
And Jezreel, and Jokdeam, and Zanoah,

(Joshua 15:57)
Cain, Gibeah, and Timnah; ten cities with their villages:

(Joshua 15:58)
Halhul, Bethzur, and Gedor,

(Joshua 15:59)
And Maarath, and Bethanoth, and Eltekon; six cities with their villages:

(Joshua 15:60)
Kirjathbaal, which is Kirjathjearim, and Rabbah; two cities with their villages:

(Joshua 15:61)
In the wilderness, Betharabah, Middin, and Secacah,

(Joshua 15:62)
And Nibshan, and the city of Salt, and Engedi; six cities with their villages.

(Joshua 15:63)
As for the Jebusites the inhabitants of Jerusalem, the children of Judah could not drive them out: but the Jebusites dwell with the children of Judah at Jerusalem to this day.

Joshua: Chapter Sixteen

(Joshua 16:1)
And the lot of the children of Joseph fell from Jordan by Jericho, to the water of Jericho on the east, to the wilderness that goes up from Jericho throughout mount Bethel,

(Joshua 16:2)
And goes out from Bethel to Luz, and passes along to the borders of Archi to Ataroth,

(Joshua 16:3)
And goes down westward to the coast of Japhleti, to the coast of Bethhoron the nether, and to Gezer: and the goings out thereof are at the sea.

(Joshua 16:4)
So the children of Joseph, Manasseh and Ephraim, took their inheritance.

(Joshua 16:5)
And the border of the children of Ephraim according to their families was thus: even the border of their inheritance on the east side was Atarothaddar, to Bethhoron the upper;

(Joshua 16:6)
And the border went out toward the sea to Michmethah on the north side; and the border went about eastward to Taanathshiloh, and passed by it on the east to Janohah;

(Joshua 16:7)
And it went down from Janohah to Ataroth, and to Naarath, and came to Jericho, and went out at Jordan.

(Joshua 16:8)
The border went out from Tappuah westward to the river Kanah; and the goings out thereof were at the sea. This is the inheritance of the tribe of the children of Ephraim by their families.

(Joshua 16:9)
And the separate cities for the children of Ephraim were among the inheritance of the children of Manasseh, all the cities with their villages.

(Joshua 16:10)
And they drove not out the Canaanites that dwelt in Gezer: but the Canaanites dwell among the Ephraimites to this day, and serve under tribute.

Joshua: Chapter Seventeen

(Joshua 17:1)

There was also a lot for the tribe of Manasseh; for he was the firstborn of Joseph; to wit, for Machir the firstborn of Manasseh, the father of Gilead: because he was a man of war, therefore he had Gilead and Bashan.

(Joshua 17:2)

There was also a lot for the rest of the children of Manasseh by their families; for the children of Abiezer, and for the children of Helek, and for the children of Asriel, and for the children of Shechem, and for the children of Hepher, and for the children of Shemida: these were the male children of Manasseh the son of Joseph by their families.

(Joshua 17:3)

But Zelophehad, the son of Hepher, the son of Gilead, the son of Machir, the son of Manasseh, had no sons, but daughters: and these are the names of his daughters, Mahlah, and Noah, Hoglah, Milcah, and Tirzah.

(Joshua 17:4)

And they came near before Eleazar the priest, and before Joshua the son of Nun, and before the princes, saying, The LORD commanded Moses to give us an inheritance among our brethren. Therefore according to the commandment of the LORD he gave them an inheritance among the brethren of their father.

(Joshua 17:5)

And there fell ten portions to Manasseh, beside the land of Gilead and Bashan, which were on the other side Jordan;

(Joshua 17:6)

Because the daughters of Manasseh had an inheritance among his sons: and the rest of Manasseh's sons had the land of Gilead.

(Joshua 17:7)

And the coast of Manasseh was from Asher to Michmethah, that lies before Shechem; and the border went along on the right hand to the inhabitants of Entappuah.

(Joshua 17:8)

Now Manasseh had the land of Tappuah: but Tappuah on the border of Manasseh belonged to the children of Ephraim;

(Joshua 17:9)

And the coast descended to the river Kanah, southward of the river: these cities of Ephraim are among the cities of Manasseh: the coast of Manasseh also was on the north side of the river, and the outgoings of it were at the sea:

(Joshua 17:10)

Southward it was Ephraim's, and northward it was Manasseh's, and the sea is his border; and they met together in Asher on the north, and in Issachar on the east.

(Joshua 17:11)

And Manasseh had in Issachar and in Asher Bethshean and her towns, and Ibleam and her towns, and the inhabitants of Dor and her towns, and the inhabitants of Endor and her towns, and the inhabitants of Taanach and her towns, and the inhabitants of Megiddo and her towns, even three countries.

(Joshua 17:12)

Yet the children of Manasseh could not drive out the inhabitants of those cities; but the Canaanites would dwell in that land.

(Joshua 17:13)

Yet it came to pass, when the children of Israel were waxen strong, that they put the Canaanites to tribute; but did not utterly drive them out.

(Joshua 17:14)

And the children of Joseph spoke to Joshua, saying, Why have you given me but one lot and one portion to inherit, seeing I am a great people, forasmuch as the LORD has blessed me up to now?

(Joshua 17:15)

And Joshua answered them, If you be a great people, then get you up to the wood country, and cut down for thyself there in the land of the Perizzites and of the giants, if mount Ephraim be too narrow for you.

(Joshua 17:16)

And the children of Joseph said, The hill is not enough for us: and all the Canaanites that dwell in the land of the valley have chariots of iron, both they who are of Bethshean and her towns, and they who are of the valley of Jezreel.

(Joshua 17:17)

And Joshua spoke to the house of Joseph, even to Ephraim and to Manasseh, saying, You are a great people, and have great power: You shall not have one lot only:

(Joshua 17:18)

But the mountain shall be your; for it is a wood, and you shall cut it down: and the outgoings of it shall be your: for you shall drive out the Canaanites, though they have iron chariots, and though they be strong.

Joshua: Chapter Eighteen

(Joshua 18:1)
And the whole congregation of the children of Israel assembled together at Shiloh, and set up the tabernacle of the congregation there. And the land was subdued before them.

(Joshua 18:2)
And there remained among the children of Israel seven tribes, which had not yet received their inheritance.

(Joshua 18:3)
And Joshua said to the children of Israel, How long are you slack to go to possess the land, which the LORD God of your fathers has given you?

(Joshua 18:4)
Give out from among you three men for each tribe: and I will send them, and they shall rise, and go through the land, and describe it according to the inheritance of them; and they shall come again to me.

(Joshua 18:5)
And they shall divide it into seven parts: Judah shall abide in their coast on the south, and the house of Joseph shall abide in their coasts on the north.

(Joshua 18:6)
You shall therefore describe the land into seven parts, and bring the description here to me, that I may cast lots for you here before the LORD our God.

(Joshua 18:7)

But the Levites have no part among you; for the priesthood of the LORD is their inheritance: and Gad, and Reuben, and half the tribe of Manasseh, have received their inheritance beyond Jordan on the east, which Moses the servant of the LORD gave them.

(Joshua 18:8)

And the men arose, and went away: and Joshua charged them that went to describe the land, saying, Go and walk through the land, and describe it, and come again to me, that I may here cast lots for you before the LORD in Shiloh.

(Joshua 18:9)

And the men went and passed through the land, and described it by cities into seven parts in a book, and came again to Joshua to the host at Shiloh.

(Joshua 18:10) (Jasher 90:19)

And Joshua cast lots for them in Shiloh before the LORD: and there Joshua divided the whole land by lots to the children of Israel according to their divisions for an inheritance, as the Lord had commanded him.

(Joshua 18:11)

And the lot of the tribe of the children of Benjamin came up according to their families: and the coast of their lot came forth between the children of Judah and the children of Joseph.

(Joshua 18:12)

And their border on the north side was from Jordan; and the border went up to the side of Jericho on the north side, and went up through the mountains westward; and the goings out thereof were at the wilderness of Bethaven.

(Joshua 18:13)

And the border went over from there toward Luz, to the side of Luz, which is Bethel, southward; and the border descended to Atarothadar, near the hill that lies on the south side of the nether Bethhoron.

(Joshua 18:14)

And the border was drawn there, and compassed the corner of the sea southward, from the hill that lies before Bethhoron southward; and the goings out thereof were at Kirjathbaal, which is Kirjathjearim, a city of the children of Judah: this was the west quarter.

(Joshua 18:15)

And the south quarter was from the end of Kirjathjearim, and the border went out on the west, and went out to the well of waters of Nephtoah:

(Joshua 18:16)

And the border came down to the end of the mountain that lies before the valley of the son of Hinnom, and which is in the valley of the giants on the north, and descended to the valley of Hinnom, to the side of Jebusi on the south, and descended to Enrogel,

(Joshua 18:17)

And was drawn from the north, and went forth to Enshemesh, and went forth toward Geliloth, which is over against the going up of Adummim, and descended to the stone of Bohan the son of Reuben,

(Joshua 18:18)

And passed along toward the side over against Arabah northward, and went down to Arabah:

(Joshua 18:19)

And the border passed along to the side of Bethhoglah northward: and the outgoings of the border were at the north bay of the salt sea at the south end of Jordan: this was the south coast.

(Joshua 18:20)

And Jordan was the border of it on the east side. This was the inheritance of the children of Benjamin, by the coasts thereof round about, according to their families.

(Joshua 18:21)

Now the cities of the tribe of the children of Benjamin according to their families were Jericho, and Bethhoglah, and the valley of Keziz,

(Joshua 18:22)

And Betharabah, and Zemaraim, and Bethel,

(Joshua 18:23)

And Avim, and Parah, and Ophrah,

(Joshua 18:24)

And Chepharhaammonai, and Ophni, and Gaba; twelve cities with their villages:

(Joshua 18:25)

Gibeon, and Ramah, and Beeroth,

(Joshua 18:26)

And Mizpeh, and Chephirah, and Mozah,

(Joshua 18:27)

And Rekem, and Irpeel, and Taralah,

(Joshua 18:28)

And Zelah, Eleph, and Jebusi, which is Jerusalem, Gibeath, and Kirjath; fourteen cities with their villages. This is the inheritance of the children of Benjamin according to their families.

Joshua: Chapter Nineteen

(Joshua 19:1)

And the second lot came forth to Simeon, even for the tribe of the children of Simeon according to their families: and their inheritance was within the inheritance of the children of Judah.

(Joshua 19:2)

And they had in their inheritance Beersheba, or Sheba, and Moladah,

(Joshua 19:3)

And Hazarshual, and Balah, and Azem,

(Joshua 19:4)

And Eltolad, and Bethul, and Hormah,

(Joshua 19:5)

And Ziklag, and Bethmarcaboth, and Hazarsusah,

(Joshua 19:6)

And Bethlebaoth, and Sharuhen; thirteen cities and their villages:

(Joshua 19:7)

Ain, Remmon, and Ether, and Ashan; four cities and their villages:

(Joshua 19:8)

And all the villages that were round about these cities to

Baalathbeer, Ramath of the south. This is the inheritance of the tribe of the children of Simeon according to their families.

(Joshua 19:9)

Out of the portion of the children of Judah was the inheritance of the children of Simeon: for the part of the children of Judah was too much for them: therefore the children of Simeon had their inheritance within the inheritance of them.

(Joshua 19:10)

And the third lot came up for the children of Zebulun according to their families: and the border of their inheritance was to Sarid:

(Joshua 19:11)

And their border went up toward the sea, and Maralah, and reached to Dabbasheth, and reached to the river that is before Jokneam;

(Joshua 19:12)

And turned from Sarid eastward toward the sunrising to the border of Chislothtabor, and then goes out to Daberath, and goes up to Japhia,

(Joshua 19:13)

And from there passes on along on the east to Gittahhepher, to Ittahkazin, and goes out to Remmonmethoar to Neah;

(Joshua 19:14)

And the border encompasses it on the north side to Hannathon: and the outgoings thereof are in the valley of Jiphthahel:

(Joshua 19:15)

And Kattath, and Nahallal, and Shimron, and Idalah, and

Bethlehem: twelve cities with their villages.

(Joshua 19:16)
This is the inheritance of the children of Zebulun according to their families, these cities with their villages.

(Joshua 19:17)
And the fourth lot came out to Issachar, for the children of Issachar according to their families.

(Joshua 19:18)
And their border was toward Jezreel, and Chesulloth, and Shunem,

(Joshua 19:19)
And Hapharaim, and Shion, and Anaharath,

(Joshua 19:20)
And Rabbith, and Kishion, and Abez,

(Joshua 19:21)
And Remeth, and Engannim, and Enhaddah, and Bethpazzez;

(Joshua 19:22)
And the coast reaches to Tabor, and Shahazimah, and Bethshemesh; and the outgoings of their border were at Jordan: sixteen cities with their villages.

(Joshua 19:23)
This is the inheritance of the tribe of the children of Issachar according to their families, the cities and their villages.

(Joshua 19:24)

And the fifth lot came out for the tribe of the children of Asher according to their families.

(Joshua 19:25)

And their border was Helkath, and Hali, and Beten, and Achshaph,

(Joshua 19:26)

And Alammelech, and Amad, and Misheal; and reaches to Carmel westward, and to Shihorlibnath;

(Joshua 19:27)

And turns toward the sunrising to Bethdagon, and reaches to Zebulun, and to the valley of Jiphthahel toward the north side of Bethemek, and Neiel, and goes out to Cabul on the left hand,

(Joshua 19:28)

And Hebron, and Rehob, and Hammon, and Kanah, even to great Zidon;

(Joshua 19:29)

And then the coast turns to Ramah, and to the strong city Tyre; and the coast turns to Hosah; and the outgoings thereof are at the sea from the coast to Achzib:

(Joshua 19:30)

Ummah also, and Aphek, and Rehob: twenty and two cities with their villages.

(Joshua 19:31)

This is the inheritance of the tribe of the children of Asher according to their families, these cities with their villages.

(Joshua 19:32)
The sixth lot came out to the children of Naphtali, even for the children of Naphtali according to their families.

(Joshua 19:33)
And their coast was from Heleph, from Allon to Zaanannim, and Adami, Nekeb, and Jabneel, to Lakum; and the outgoings thereof were at Jordan:

(Joshua 19:34)
And then the coast turns westward to Aznothtabor, and goes out from there to Hukkok, and reaches to Zebulun on the south side, and reaches to Asher on the west side, and to Judah upon Jordan toward the sunrising.

(Joshua 19:35)
And the fenced cities are Ziddim, Zer, and Hammath, Rakkath, and Chinnereth,

(Joshua 19:36)
And Adamah, and Ramah, and Hazor,

(Joshua 19:37)
And Kedesh, and Edrei, and Enhazor,

(Joshua 19:38)
And Iron, and Migdalel, Horem, and Bethanath, and Bethshemesh; nineteen cities with their villages.

(Joshua 19:39)
This is the inheritance of the tribe of the children of Naphtali according to their families, the cities and their villages.

(Joshua 19:40)
And the seventh lot came out for the tribe of the children of Dan according to their families.

(Joshua 19:41)
And the coast of their inheritance was Zorah, and Eshtaol, and Irshemesh,

(Joshua 19:42)
And Shaalabbin, and Ajalon, and Jethlah,

(Joshua 19:43)
And Elon, and Thimnathah, and Ekron,

(Joshua 19:44)
And Eltekeh, and Gibbethon, and Baalath,

(Joshua 19:45)
And Jehud, and Beneberak, and Gathrimmon,

(Joshua 19:46)
And Mejarkon, and Rakkon, with the border before Japho.

(Joshua 19:47)
And the coast of the children of Dan went out too little for them: therefore the children of Dan went up to fight against Leshem, and took it, and smote it with the edge of the sword, and possessed it, and dwelt therein, and called Leshem, Dan, after the name of Dan their father.

(Joshua 19:48)
This is the inheritance of the tribe of the children of Dan according to their families, these cities with their villages.

(Joshua 19:49...)

When they had made an end of dividing the land for inheritance by their coasts.

(...Joshua 19:49) (Jasher 90:21)

And they went to inherit the land according to their boundaries, and the children of Israel gave an inheritance to Joshua the son of Nun among them:

(Joshua 19:50) (Jasher 90:22)

According to the word of the LORD they gave him the city which he asked, even Timnathserah in mount Ephraim: and he built the city, and dwelt therein.

(Joshua 19:51) (Jasher 90:23)

These are the inheritances, which Eleazar the priest, and Joshua the son of Nun, and the heads of the fathers of the tribes of the children of Israel, divided for an inheritance and portioned out to the children of Israel by lot in Shiloh before the LORD, at the door of the tabernacle of the congregation. So they made an end of dividing the country.

(Jasher 90:23)

And Joshua called to all the children of Israel and he blessed them, and commanded them to serve the Lord, and he afterward sent them away, and they went each man to his city, and each man to his inheritance.

Joshua: Chapter Twenty

(Joshua 20:1)
The LORD also spoke to Joshua, saying,

(Joshua 20:2)
Speak to the children of Israel, saying, Appoint out for you cities of refuge, whereof I spoke to you by the hand of Moses:

(Joshua 20:3)
That the slayer that kills any person unawares and unwittingly may flee there: and they shall be your refuge from the avenger of blood.

(Joshua 20:4)
And when he that doth flee to one of those cities shall stand at the entering of the gate of the city, and shall declare his cause in the ears of the elders of that city, they shall take him into the city to them, and give him a place, that he may dwell among them.

(Joshua 20:5)
And if the avenger of blood pursue after him, then they shall not deliver the slayer up into his hand; because he smote his neighbor unwittingly, and hated him not previously.

(Joshua 20:6)
And he shall dwell in that city, until he stand before the congregation for judgment, and until the death of the high priest that shall be in those days: then shall the slayer return,

and come to his own city, and to his own house, to the city from where he fled.

(Joshua 20:7)

And they appointed Kedesh in Galilee in mount Naphtali, and Shechem in mount Ephraim, and Kirjatharba, which is Hebron, in the mountain of Judah.

(Joshua 20:8)

And on the other side Jordan by Jericho eastward, they assigned Bezer in the wilderness upon the plain out of the tribe of Reuben, and Ramoth in Gilead out of the tribe of Gad, and Golan in Bashan out of the tribe of Manasseh.

(Joshua 20:9)

These were the cities appointed for all the children of Israel, and for the stranger that sojourns among them, that whosoever kills any person at unawares might flee there, and not die by the hand of the avenger of blood, until he stood before the congregation.

Joshua: Chapter Twenty-One

(Joshua 21:1)

Then came near the heads of the fathers of the Levites to Eleazar the priest, and to Joshua the son of Nun, and to the heads of the fathers of the tribes of the children of Israel;

(Joshua 21:2)

And they spoke to them at Shiloh in the land of Canaan, saying, The LORD commanded by the hand of Moses to give us cities to dwell in, with the suburbs thereof for our cattle.

(Joshua 21:3) (Jasher 90:20...)

And the children of Israel gave to the Levites out of their inheritance, at the commandment of the LORD, these cities and their suburbs for their cattle, and property.

(Joshua 21:4)

And the lot came out for the families of the Kohathites: and the children of Aaron the priest, which were of the Levites, had by lot out of the tribe of Judah, and out of the tribe of Simeon, and out of the tribe of Benjamin, thirteen cities.

(Joshua 21:5)

And the rest of the children of Kohath had by lot out of the families of the tribe of Ephraim, and out of the tribe of Dan, and out of the half tribe of Manasseh, ten cities.

(Joshua 21:6)

And the children of Gershon had by lot out of the families of the tribe of Issachar, and out of the tribe of Asher, and out of the tribe of Naphtali, and out of the half tribe of Manasseh in Bashan, thirteen cities.

(Joshua 21:7)

The children of Merari by their families had out of the tribe of Reuben, and out of the tribe of Gad, and out of the tribe of Zebulun, twelve cities.

(Joshua 21:8) (Jasher 90:20)

And the children of Israel gave by lot to the Levites these cities with their suburbs, as the LORD commanded by the hand of Moses, so did the children of Israel, and they divided the land by lot whether great or small.

(Joshua 21:9)

And they gave out of the tribe of the children of Judah, and out of the tribe of the children of Simeon, these cities which are here mentioned by name,

(Joshua 21:10)

Which the children of Aaron, being of the families of the Kohathites, who were of the children of Levi, had: for theirs was the first lot.

(Joshua 21:11)

And they gave them the city of Arba the father of Anak, which city is Hebron, in the hill country of Judah, with the suburbs thereof round about it.

(Joshua 21:12)

But the fields of the city, and the villages thereof, gave they to Caleb the son of Jephunneh for his possession.

(Joshua 21:13)
Thus they gave to the children of Aaron the priest Hebron with her suburbs, to be a city of refuge for the slayer; and Libnah with her suburbs,

(Joshua 21:14)
And Jattir with her suburbs, and Eshtemoa with her suburbs,

(Joshua 21:15)
And Holon with her suburbs, and Debir with her suburbs,

(Joshua 21:16)
And Ain with her suburbs, and Juttah with her suburbs, and Bethshemesh with her suburbs; nine cities out of those two tribes.

(Joshua 21:17)
And out of the tribe of Benjamin, Gibeon with her suburbs, Geba with her suburbs,

(Joshua 21:18)
Anathoth with her suburbs, and Almon with her suburbs; four cities.

(Joshua 21:19)
All the cities of the children of Aaron, the priests, were thirteen cities with their suburbs.

(Joshua 21:20)
And the families of the children of Kohath, the Levites which remained of the children of Kohath, even they had the cities of their lot out of the tribe of Ephraim.

(Joshua 21:21)

For they gave them Shechem with her suburbs in mount Ephraim, to be a city of refuge for the slayer; and Gezer with her suburbs,

(Joshua 21:22)

And Kibzaim with her suburbs, and Bethhoron with her suburbs; four cities.

(Joshua 21:23)

And out of the tribe of Dan, Eltekeh with her suburbs, Gibbethon with her suburbs,

(Joshua 21:24)

Aijalon with her suburbs, Gathrimmon with her suburbs; four cities.

(Joshua 21:25)

And out of the half tribe of Manasseh, Tanach with her suburbs, and Gathrimmon with her suburbs; two cities.

(Joshua 21:26)

All the cities were ten with their suburbs for the families of the children of Kohath that remained.

(Joshua 21:27)

And to the children of Gershon, of the families of the Levites, out of the other half tribe of Manasseh they gave Golan in Bashan with her suburbs, to be a city of refuge for the slayer; and Beeshterah with her suburbs; two cities.

(Joshua 21:28)

And out of the tribe of Issachar, Kishon with her suburbs, Dabareh with her suburbs,

(Joshua 21:29)
Jarmuth with her suburbs, Engannim with her suburbs; four cities.

(Joshua 21:30)
And out of the tribe of Asher, Mishal with her suburbs, Abdon with her suburbs,

(Joshua 21:31)
Helkath with her suburbs, and Rehob with her suburbs; four cities.

(Joshua 21:32)
And out of the tribe of Naphtali, Kedesh in Galilee with her suburbs, to be a city of refuge for the slayer; and Hammothdor with her suburbs, and Kartan with her suburbs; three cities.

(Joshua 21:33)
All the cities of the Gershonites according to their families were thirteen cities with their suburbs.

(Joshua 21:34)
And to the families of the children of Merari, the rest of the Levites, out of the tribe of Zebulun, Jokneam with her suburbs, and Kartah with her suburbs,

(Joshua 21:35)
Dimnah with her suburbs, Nahalal with her suburbs; four cities.

(Joshua 21:36)
And out of the tribe of Reuben, Bezer with her suburbs, and Jahazah with her suburbs,

(Joshua 21:37)

Kedemoth with her suburbs, and Mephaath with her suburbs; four cities.

(Joshua 21:38)

And out of the tribe of Gad, Ramoth in Gilead with her suburbs, to be a city of refuge for the slayer; and Mahanaim with her suburbs,

(Joshua 21:39)

Heshbon with her suburbs, Jazer with her suburbs; four cities in all.

(Joshua 21:40)

So all the cities for the children of Merari by their families, which were remaining of the families of the Levites, were by their lot twelve cities.

(Joshua 21:41)

All the cities of the Levites within the possession of the children of Israel were forty and eight cities with their suburbs.

(Joshua 21:42)

These cities were every one with their suburbs round about them: thus were all these cities.

(Joshua 21:43) (Jasher 90:24)

And the LORD gave to Israel all the land which he had spoken to them and as the Lord had swore to give to their fathers; and they possessed it, and dwelt therein.

(Joshua 21:44) (Jasher 90:25..., 27)

And the children of Israel served the Lord all the days of Joshua, and the LORD gave them rest from all their enemies round about, according to all that he swore to their fathers: and there stood not a man of all their enemies before them; the LORD delivered all their enemies into their hand, and they dwelt securely in their cities.

(Joshua 21:45) (...Jasher 90:25)

There failed not ought of any good thing which the LORD had spoken to the house of Israel; all came to pass, yea, the Lord performed every thing.

Joshua: Chapter Twenty-Two

(Joshua 22:1)
Then Joshua called the Reubenites, and the Gadites, and the half tribe of Manasseh,

(Joshua 22:2)
And said to them, You have kept all that Moses the servant of the LORD commanded you, and have obeyed my voice in all that I commanded you:

(Joshua 22:3)
You have not left your brethren these many days to this day, but have kept the charge of the commandment of the LORD your God.

(Joshua 22:4)
And now the LORD your God has given rest to your brethren, as he promised them: therefore now return you, and get you to your tents, and to the land of your possession, which Moses the servant of the LORD gave you on the other side Jordan.

(Joshua 22:5)
But take diligent heed to do the commandment and the law, which Moses the servant of the LORD charged you, to love the LORD your God, and to walk in all his ways, and to keep his commandments, and to cleave to him, and to serve him with all your heart and with all your soul.

(Joshua 22:6)

So Joshua blessed them, and sent them away: and they went to their tents.

(Joshua 22:7)

Now to the one half of the tribe of Manasseh Moses had given possession in Bashan: but to the other half thereof gave Joshua among their brethren on this side Jordan westward. And when Joshua sent them away also to their tents, then he blessed them,

(Joshua 22:8)

And he spoke to them, saying, Return with much riches to your tents, and with very much cattle, with silver, and with gold, and with brass, and with iron, and with very much raiment: divide the spoil of your enemies with your brethren.

(Joshua 22:9)

And the children of Reuben and the children of Gad and the half tribe of Manasseh returned, and departed from the children of Israel out of Shiloh, which is in the land of Canaan, to go to the country of Gilead, to the land of their possession, whereof they were possessed, according to the word of the LORD by the hand of Moses.

(Joshua 22:10)

And when they came to the borders of Jordan, that are in the land of Canaan, the children of Reuben and the children of Gad and the half tribe of Manasseh built there an altar by Jordan, a great altar to see to.

(Joshua 22:11)

And the children of Israel heard say, Behold, the children of Reuben and the children of Gad and the half tribe of Manasseh have built an altar over against the land of Canaan, in the borders of Jordan, at the passage of the children of Israel.

(Joshua 22:12)

And when the children of Israel heard of it, the whole congregation of the children of Israel gathered themselves together at Shiloh, to go up to war against them.

(Joshua 22:13)

And the children of Israel sent to the children of Reuben, and to the children of Gad, and to the half tribe of Manasseh, into the land of Gilead, Phinehas the son of Eleazar the priest,

(Joshua 22:14)

And with him ten princes, of each chief house a prince throughout all the tribes of Israel; and each one was an head of the house of their fathers among the thousands of Israel.

(Joshua 22:15)

And they came to the children of Reuben, and to the children of Gad, and to the half tribe of Manasseh, to the land of Gilead, and they spoke with them, saying,

(Joshua 22:16)

Thus saith the whole congregation of the LORD, What trespass is this that you have committed against the God of Israel, to turn away this day from following the LORD, in that you have built an altar, that you might rebel this day against the LORD?

(Joshua 22:17)

Is the iniquity of Peor too little for us, from which we are not cleansed until this day, although there was a plague in the congregation of the LORD,

(Joshua 22:18)

But that you must turn away this day from following the LORD? And it will be, seeing you rebel to day against the LORD, that to morrow he will be wroth with the whole congregation of Israel.

(Joshua 22:19)

Notwithstanding, if the land of your possession be unclean, then pass you over to the land of the possession of the LORD, wherein the LORD'S tabernacle dwells, and take possession among us: but rebel not against the LORD, nor rebel against us, in building you an altar beside the altar of the LORD our God.

(Joshua 22:20)

Did not Achan the son of Zerah commit a trespass in the accursed thing, and wrath fell on all the congregation of Israel? And that man perished not alone in his iniquity.

(Joshua 22:21)

Then the children of Reuben and the children of Gad and the half tribe of Manasseh answered, and said to the heads of the thousands of Israel,

(Joshua 22:22)

The LORD God of gods, the LORD God of gods, he knows, and Israel he shall know; if it be in rebellion, or if in transgression against the LORD, (save us not this day,)

(Joshua 22:23)

That we have built us an altar to turn from following the LORD, or if to offer thereon burnt offering or meat offering, or if to offer peace offerings thereon, let the LORD himself require it;

(Joshua 22:24)

And if we have not rather done it for fear of this thing, saying, In time to come your children might speak to our children, saying, What have you to do with the LORD God of Israel?

(Joshua 22:25)

For the LORD has made Jordan a border between us and you, you children of Reuben and children of Gad; you have no part in the LORD: so shall your children make our children cease from fearing the LORD.

(Joshua 22:26)

Therefore we said, Let us now prepare to build us an altar, not for burnt offering, nor for sacrifice:

(Joshua 22:27)

But that it may be a witness between us, and you, and our generations after us, that we might do the service of the LORD before him with our burnt offerings, and with our sacrifices, and with our peace offerings; that your children may not say to our children in time to come, you have no part in the LORD.

(Joshua 22:28)

Therefore said we, that it shall be, when they should so say to us or to our generations in time to come, that we may say again, Behold the pattern of the altar of the LORD, which our fathers made, not for burnt offerings, nor for sacrifices; but it is a witness between us and you.

(Joshua 22:29)

God forbid that we should rebel against the LORD, and turn this day from following the LORD, to build an altar for burnt offerings, for meat offerings, or for sacrifices, beside the altar of the LORD our God that is before his tabernacle.

(Joshua 22:30)

And when Phinehas the priest, and the princes of the congregation and heads of the thousands of Israel which were with him, heard the words that the children of Reuben and the children of Gad and the children of Manasseh spoke, it pleased them.

(Joshua 22:31)

And Phinehas the son of Eleazar the priest said to the children of Reuben, and to the children of Gad, and to the children of Manasseh, This day we perceive that the LORD is among us, because you have not committed this trespass against the LORD: now you have delivered the children of Israel out of the hand of the LORD.

(Joshua 22:32)

And Phinehas the son of Eleazar the priest, and the princes, returned from the children of Reuben, and from the children of Gad, out of the land of Gilead, to the land of Canaan, to the children of Israel, and brought them word again.

(Joshua 22:33)

And the thing pleased the children of Israel; and the children of Israel blessed God, and did not intend to go up against them in battle, to destroy the land wherein the children of Reuben and Gad dwelt.

(Joshua 22:34)

And the children of Reuben and the children of Gad called the altar Ed: for it shall be a witness between us that the LORD is God.

Joshua: Chapter Twenty-Three

(Jasher 90:28)
And it came to pass in those days, that Abianus king of Chittim died, in the thirty-eighth year of his reign, that is the seventh year of his reign over Edom, and they buried him in his place which he had built for himself, and Latinus reigned in his stead fifty years.

(Jasher 90:29)
And during his reign he brought forth an army, and he went and fought against the inhabitants of Britannia and Kernania, the children of Elisha son of Javan, and he prevailed over them and made them tributary.

(Jasher 90:30)
He then heard that Edom had revolted from under the hand of Chittim, and Latinus went to them and smote them and subdued them, and placed them under the hand of the children of Chittim, and Edom became one kingdom with the children of Chittim all the days.

(Jasher 90:31)
And for many years there was no king in Edom, and their government was with the children of Chittim and their king.

(Joshua 23:1) (Jasher 90:32)
And it came to pass a long time after that the LORD had given rest to Israel from all their enemies round about, it was in the twenty-sixth year after the children of Israel had passed the Jordan, that is the sixty-sixth year after the children of Israel

had departed from Egypt, that Joshua waxed old and stricken in age, being one hundred and eight years old in those days.

(Joshua 23:2) (Jasher 90:33...)

And Joshua called for all Israel, and for their elders, and for their heads, and for their judges, and for their officers after the Lord had given to all the Israelites rest from all their enemies round about, and Joshua said to them, to the elders of Israel, and to their judges, I am old and stricken in age:

(Joshua 23:3) (...Jasher 90:33)

And you have seen all that the LORD your God has done to all these nations whom he has driven away from before you, because of you; for the LORD your God is he that has fought for you.

(Joshua 23:4)

Behold, I have divided to you by lot these nations that remain, to be an inheritance for your tribes, from Jordan, with all the nations that I have cut off, even to the great sea westward.

(Joshua 23:5)

And the LORD your God, he shall expel them from before you, and drive them from out of your sight; and you shall possess their land, as the LORD your God has promised to you.

(Joshua 23:6) (Jasher 90:34...)

Now therefore, be therefore very courageous, strengthen yourselves to keep and to do all that is written in the book, all the words of the law of Moses, that you turn not aside therefrom to deviate from it to the right hand or to the left;

(Joshua 23:7) (...Jasher 90:34...)

That you come not among these nations, these that remain in

the land among you; neither shall you make mention of the name of their gods, nor cause to swear by them, neither serve them, nor bow yourselves to them:

(Joshua 23:8) (...Jasher 90:34)
But cleave to the LORD your God, as you have done to this day.

(Joshua 23:9)
For the LORD has driven out from before you great nations and strong: but as for you, no man has been able to stand before you to this day.

(Joshua 23:10)
One man of you shall chase a thousand: for the LORD your God, he it is that fights for you, as he has promised you.

(Joshua 23:11)
Take good heed therefore to yourselves, that you love the LORD your God.

(Joshua 23:12)
Else if you do in any wise go back, and cleave to the remnant of these nations, even these that remain among you, and shall make marriages with them, and go in to them, and they to you:

(Joshua 23:13)
Know for a certainty that the LORD your God will no more drive out any of these nations from before you; but they shall be snares and traps to you, and scourges in your sides, and thorns in your eyes, until you perish from off this good land which the LORD your God has given you.

(Joshua 23:14)

And, behold, this day I am going the way of all the earth: and you know in all your hearts and in all your souls, that not one thing has failed of all the good things which the LORD your God spoke concerning you; all are come to pass to you, and not one thing has failed thereof.

(Joshua 23:15)

Therefore it shall come to pass, that as all good things are come upon you, which the LORD your God promised you; so shall the LORD bring upon you all evil things, until he have destroyed you from off this good land which the LORD your God has given you.

(Joshua 23:16)

When you have transgressed the covenant of the LORD your God, which he commanded you, and have gone and served other gods, and bowed yourselves to them; then shall the anger of the LORD be kindled against you, and you shall perish quickly from off the good land which he has given to you.

Joshua: Chapter Twenty-Four

(Joshua 24:1)

And Joshua gathered all the tribes of Israel to Shechem, and called for the elders of Israel, and for their heads, and for their judges, and for their officers; and they presented themselves before God.

(Joshua 24:2)

And Joshua said to all the people, Thus saith the LORD God of Israel, Your fathers dwelt on the other side of the flood in old time, even Terah, the father of Abraham, and the father of Nachor: and they served other gods.

(Joshua 24:3)

And I took your father Abraham from the other side of the flood, and led him throughout all the land of Canaan, and multiplied his seed, and gave him Isaac.

(Joshua 24:4)

And I gave to Isaac Jacob and Esau: and I gave to Esau mount Seir, to possess it; but Jacob and his children went down into Egypt.

(Joshua 24:5)

I sent Moses also and Aaron, and I plagued Egypt, according to that which I did among them: and afterward I brought you out.

(Joshua 24:6)

And I brought your fathers out of Egypt: and you came to

the sea; and the Egyptians pursued after your fathers with chariots and horsemen to the Red sea.

(Joshua 24:7)
And when they cried to the LORD, he put darkness between you and the Egyptians, and brought the sea upon them, and covered them; and your eyes have seen what I have done in Egypt: and you dwelt in the wilderness a long season.

(Joshua 24:8)
And I brought you into the land of the Amorites, which dwelt on the other side Jordan; and they fought with you: and I gave them into your hand, that you might possess their land; and I destroyed them from before you.

(Joshua 24:9)
Then Balak the son of Zippor, king of Moab, arose and warred against Israel, and sent and called Balaam the son of Beor to curse you:

(Joshua 24:10)
But I would not hearken to Balaam; therefore he blessed you still: so I delivered you out of his hand.

(Joshua 24:11)
And you went over Jordan, and came to Jericho: and the men of Jericho fought against you, the Amorites, and the Perizzites, and the Canaanites, and the Hittites, and the Girgashites, the Hivites, and the Jebusites; and I delivered them into your hand.

(Joshua 24:12)
And I sent the hornet before you, which drove them out from before you, even the two kings of the Amorites; but not with

your sword, nor with your bow.

(Joshua 24:13)

And I have given you a land for which you did not labor, and cities which you built not, and you dwell in them; of the vineyards and olive yards which you planted not do you eat.

(Joshua 24:14)

Now therefore fear the LORD, and serve him in sincerity and in truth: and put away the gods which your fathers served on the other side of the flood, and in Egypt; and serve you the LORD.

(Joshua 24:15)

And if it seem evil to you to serve the LORD, choose you this day whom you will serve; whether the gods which your fathers served that were on the other side of the flood, or the gods of the Amorites, in whose land you dwell: but as for me and my house, we will serve the LORD.

(Joshua 24:16)

And the people answered and said, God forbid that we should forsake the LORD, to serve other gods;

(Joshua 24:17)

For the LORD our God, he it is that brought us up and our fathers out of the land of Egypt, from the house of bondage, and which did those great signs in our sight, and preserved us in all the way wherein we went, and among all the people through whom we passed:

(Joshua 24:18)

And the LORD drove out from before us all the people, even the Amorites which dwelt in the land: therefore will we also serve the LORD; for he is our God.

(Joshua 24:19)

And Joshua said to the people, You cannot serve the LORD: for he is an holy God; he is a jealous God; he will not forgive your transgressions nor your sins.

(Joshua 24:20)

If you forsake the LORD, and serve strange gods, then he will turn and do you hurt, and consume you, after that he has done you good.

(Joshua 24:21)

And the people said to Joshua, Nay; but we will serve the LORD.

(Joshua 24:22)

And Joshua said to the people, You are witnesses against yourselves that you have chosen you the LORD, to serve him. And they said, We are witnesses.

(Joshua 24:23)

Now therefore put away, said he, the strange gods which are among you, and incline your heart to the LORD God of Israel.

(Jasher 90:35)

And Joshua greatly exhorted the children of Israel to serve the Lord all their days.

(Joshua 24:24) (Jasher 90:36)

And all the people of Israel said to Joshua, The LORD our God will we serve, and his voice will we obey all our days, we and our children, and our children's children, and our seed forever.

(Joshua 24:25) (Jasher 90:37...)

So Joshua made a covenant with the people that day, and set them a statute and an ordinance in Shechem.

(Joshua 24:26)

And Joshua wrote these words in the book of the law of God, and took a great stone, and set it up there under an oak, that was by the sanctuary of the LORD.

(Joshua 24:27)

And Joshua said to all the people, Behold, this stone shall be a witness to us; for it has heard all the words of the LORD which he spoke to us: it shall be therefore a witness to you, lest you deny your God.

(Joshua 24:28) (...Jasher 90:37)

So Joshua sent away the children of Israel and let the people depart, and they went every man to his inheritance and to his city.

(Jasher 90:38)
And it was in those days, when the children of Israel were dwelling securely in their cities, that they buried the coffins of the tribes of their ancestors, which they had brought up from Egypt, each man in the inheritance of his children, the twelve sons of Jacob did the children of Israel bury, each man in the possession of his children.

(Jasher 90:39)
And these are the names of the cities wherein they buried the twelve sons of Jacob, whom the children of Israel had brought up from Egypt.

(Jasher 90:40)
And they buried Reuben and Gad on this side Jordan, in Romia, which Moses had given to their children.

(Jasher 90:41)
And Simeon and Levi they buried in the city Mauda, which he had given to the children of Simeon, and the suburb of the city was for the children of Levi.

(Jasher 90:42)
And Judah they buried in the city of Benjamin opposite Bethlehem.

(Jasher 90:43)
And the bones of Issachar and Zebulun they buried in Zidon, in the portion which fell to their children.

(Jasher 90:44)
And Dan was buried in the city of his children in Eshtael, and Naphtali and Asher they buried in Kadesh-naphtali, each man in his place which he had given to his children.

(Jasher 90:45)
And the bones of Joseph they buried in Shechem, in the part of the field which Jacob had purchased from Hamor, and which became to Joseph for an inheritance.

(Jasher 90:46)
And they buried Benjamin in Jerusalem opposite the Jebusite, which was given to the children of Benjamin; the children of Israel buried their fathers each man in the city of his children.

(Joshua 24:29) (Jasher 90:47)
And it came to pass after these things, at the end of two years,

that Joshua the son of Nun, the servant of the LORD, died, being an hundred and ten years old, and the time which Joshua judged Israel was twenty-eight years, and Israel served the Lord all the days of his life.

(Jasher 90:48)
And the other affairs of Joshua and his battles and his reproofs with which he reproved Israel, and all which he had commanded them, and the names of the cities which the children of Israel possessed in his days, behold they are written in the book of the words of Joshua to the children of Israel, and in the book of the wars of the Lord, which Moses and Joshua and the children of Israel had written.

(Joshua 24:30) (Jasher 90:49)
And the children of Israel buried him in the border of his inheritance in Timnathserah, which is in mount Ephraim, on the north side of the hill of Gaash.

(Joshua 24:31)
And Israel served the LORD all the days of Joshua, and all the days of the elders that overlived Joshua, and which had known all the works of the LORD, that he had done for Israel.

(Joshua 24:32)
And the bones of Joseph, which the children of Israel brought up out of Egypt, buried they in Shechem, in a parcel of ground which Jacob bought of the sons of Hamor the father of Shechem for an hundred pieces of silver: and it became the inheritance of the children of Joseph.

(Joshua 24:33) (Jasher 90:50)
And Eleazar the son of Aaron died in those days; and they buried him in a hill that pertained to Phinehas his son, which was given him in mount Ephraim.

~ ~ ~

(Jasher 91:1)
At that time, after the death of Joshua, the children of the Canaanites were still in the land, and the Israelites resolved to drive them out.

(Jasher 91:2)
And the children of Israel asked of the Lord, saying, Who shall first go up for us to the Canaanites to fight against them? And the Lord said, Judah shall go up.

(Jasher 91:3)
And the children of Judah said to Simeon, Go up with us into our lot, and we will fight against the Canaanites and we likewise will go up with you, in your lot, so the children of Simeon went with the children of Judah.

(Jasher 91:4)
And the children of Judah went up and fought against the Canaanites, so the Lord delivered the Canaanites into the hands of the children of Judah, and they smote them in Bezek, ten thousand men.

(Jasher 91:5)
And they fought with Adonibezek in Bezek, and he fled from before them, and they pursued him and caught him, and they took hold of him and cut off his thumbs and great toes.

(Jasher 91:6)
And Adonibezek said, Three score and ten kings having their

thumbs and great toes cut off, gathered their meat under my table, as I have done, so God has requited me, and they brought him to Jerusalem and he died there.

(Jasher 91:7)
And the children of Simeon went with the children of Judah, and they smote the Canaanites with the edge of the sword.

(Jasher 91:8)
And the Lord was with the children of Judah, and they possessed the mountain, and the children of Joseph went up to Bethel, the same is Luz, and the Lord was with them.

(Jasher 91:9)
And the children of Joseph spied out Bethel, and the watchmen saw a man going forth from the city, and they caught him and said to him, Show us now the entrance of the city and we will show kindness to you.

(Jasher 91:10)
And that man showed them the entrance of the city, and the children of Joseph came and smote the City with the edge of the sword.

(Jasher 91:11)
And the man with his family they sent away, and he went to the Hittites and he built a city, and he called the name thereof Luz, so all the Israelites dwelt in their cities, and the children at Israel dwelt in their cities, and the children of Israel served the Lord all the days of Joshua, and all the days of the elders, who had lengthened their days after Joshua, and saw the great work of the Lord, which he had performed for Israel.

(Jasher 91:12)
And the elders judged Israel after the death of Joshua for seventeen years.

(Jasher 91:13)
And all the elders also fought the battles of Israel against the Canaanites and the Lord drove the Canaanites from before the children of Israel, in order to place the Israelites in their land.

(Jasher 91:14)
And he accomplished all the words which he had spoken to Abraham, Isaac, and Jacob, and the oath which he had sworn, to give to them and to their children, the land of the Canaanites.

(Jasher 91:15)
And the Lord gave to the children of Israel the whole land of Canaan, as he had sworn to their ancestors, and the Lord gave them rest from those around them, and the children of Israel dwelt securely in their cities.

(Jasher 91:16)
Blessed be the Lord for ever, amen, and amen.

(Jasher 91:17)
Strengthen yourselves, and let the hearts of all you that trust in the Lord be of good courage.

Epilogue

(Enoch 91:1)
That which was written by Enoch. He wrote all this instruction of wisdom for every man of dignity, and every judge of the earth; for all my children who shall dwell upon earth, and for subsequent generations, conducting themselves uprightly and peaceably.

(Enoch 91:2)
Let not your spirit be grieved on account of the times; for the Holy, the Great One, has prescribed a period to all.

(Enoch 91:3)
Let the righteous man arise from slumber; let him arise, and proceed in the path of righteousness, in all its paths; and let him advance in goodness and in eternal clemency. Mercy shall be showed to the righteous man; upon him shall be conferred integrity and power forever. In goodness and in righteousness shall he exist, and shall walk in everlasting light; but sin shall perish in eternal darkness, nor be seen from this time forward forevermore.

(Conclusion of the Book of Enoch)

Here ends the vision of Enoch the prophet. May the benediction of his prayer, and the gift of his appointed period, be with his beloved! Amen.

Final Notes

We hope your journey is enriched and you are blessed through the production of the **Ancient Texts and the Bible** series!

Minister 2 Others would like to hear from you. If you have comments or questions concerning our materials, or if you find errors in our projects, misspellings, or formatting issues. We work hard to provide quality materials, however, sometimes things can squeak by unnoticed. Your feedback is truly appreciated.

We love producing helpful, innovative books and we are grateful for your support! If you have enjoyed this production, please consider writing a review and letting others know about our materials.

If you would like to be updated when we release new books and other materials, please sign up for our e-newsletter on our website.

Thanks!

Minister 2 Others

Minister2others.com

www.ingramcontent.com/pod-product-compliance
Lightning Source LLC
Chambersburg PA
CBHW060752210726
48292CB00014B/2791

* 9 7 8 1 9 4 7 7 5 1 3 9 2 *